Tusshar Kapoor is an Indian film actor and producer. He studied at the Bombay Scottish School before moving to the US for higher studies. He has a bachelor's degree in business administration from the University of Michigan and worked as a financial analyst with an American automotive company before returning to India to pursue a career in entertainment.

Tusshar's acting journey began in 2001 with the hit film *Mujhe Kucch Kehna Hai*. Since then, he has appeared in hits like *Khakee*, *The Dirty Picture*, *Shootout at Lokhandwala* and *Shor in the City*, among others. His impeccable comic timing as a mute character in the blockbuster comic franchise *Golmaal* made him a household name and a favourite among kids and families.

Tusshar is the son of veteran actor Jeetendra. After completing twenty years in the film industry, he donned the hat of a producer with the horror–comedy *Laxmii*. His next production venture is a mystery thriller titled *Maarich*.

This is his first book.

BACHELOR DAD

MY JOURNEY TO FATHERHOOD AND MORE

TUSSHAR KAPOOR

EBURY
PRESS

An imprint of Penguin Random House

EBURY PRESS

USA | Canada | UK | Ireland | Australia
New Zealand | India | South Africa | China

Ebury Press is part of the Penguin Random House group of companies
whose addresses can be found at global.penguinrandomhouse.com

Published by Penguin Random House India Pvt. Ltd
4th Floor, Capital Tower 1, MG Road,
Gurugram 122 002, Haryana, India

Penguin
Random House
India

First published in Ebury Press by Penguin Random House India 2022

ISBN 9780143452898

Typeset in Adobe Garamond Pro by Manipal Technologies Limited, Manipal
Printed at Replika Press Pvt. Ltd, India

www.penguin.co.in

To all single moms and dads—
it's twice the work, twice the tears,
but it's also twice the hugs and love

Contents

The Beginning of a Maze   1

Divine Intervention   23

A Marriage of Beautiful Minds   47

The Arrival of a New Dawn   69

Baby Steps into a New Normal   89

The Wheels of Our Bus Start to Go Round   111

When Reality Bites   135

A Roller-coaster Year   157

The Invisible Enemy and the Lockdown   181

And Miles to Go Before We Really Unlock   205

Epilogue   228

Acknowledgements   230

The Beginning of a Maze

As I begin writing my first book, which talks about a certain aspect of my adult life, I'm reminded of the same feelings that surfaced when I stood at the brink of adulthood—feelings of uncertainty, curiosity and a slight nervousness about what lay ahead. Back in 2012, I remember going to bed wondering what was in store for me as far as my family life was concerned. 'I'm thirty-five and single. Do I want to get married soon? Yes, I would love to be a father someday, so do I need to give up my independence as a bachelor?' Today, as I share my thoughts and experiences as a single father, a 'bachelor dad', I'm a little nervous. I've never written a book before—how am I going to do it? Will it be worth reading and, most importantly, where do I even begin?

The solution to my bewilderment was never planned or crafted out. First, I would never even think about 'arranging' a marriage for myself, despite knowing that my family would put their best foot forward for me . . . That's just how I am, how I have always been. In the past, too, I have never let friends and relatives have too much of a say in my choice of field of education, where and at which university abroad I studied, how I managed to get my first job as a financial analyst and, eventually, why I left an opportunity in the corporate world in the US to come back to India and pursue a career in Hindi films.

Fortunately, I was allowed to find my own calling and pursue a career of my own liking, a daunting task for someone who had never been exposed to the professional world outside of the movies. I worked hard to graduate with an honours degree in finance from the University of Michigan, Ann Arbor, but struggled to find a job that would make me want to settle down in the corporate world for life. Perhaps my heart was drawn to the movies, and I returned to India, confident about myself but confused about which part of filmmaking I felt most passionately about. I tried to find my bearings with a stint as an assistant director and then landed my first job as an actor. I got that through the networking I did on my set—luck, of course—and I'd like to believe it was a reward for my having braved through several storms before finding something that felt close to my heart. Contrary to popular opinion about the lives of star sons, my journey into Bollywood was quite challenging and, most importantly, my own. So, I thought years later, if I can struggle, introspect and find an independent career choice for myself, then that is how I'm going to make a family, too. One that is my own, one that I trust and one that I would sacrifice anything for.

On nights when I wasn't obsessing over movies and my professional commitments, a silent realization was beginning to grow in the back of my mind. A realization that probably hits everyone who's as carefree and nonchalant about personal life choices as me—that as a man, you can get married later in life, but you can't wait very long to have children if you want to be a young, energetic and engaged father . . . in case I was seriously wanting to be one at some point in my life.

Also, no matter how much I skirted this issue during casual family conversations, there was ample evidence—a definite vibe—that my parents were getting restless. Restless about their status as non-grandparents. There was pressure being mounted in different ways, some which I had never anticipated. My first serious and close encounter with this pressure was the experience of having to deal with a proposal for an arranged marriage. Of course, it had to be someone I'd never met, someone far removed from my line of work, and the rest of it had to unfold if and when I agreed to take up the offer of at least a meeting in person with this girl of their choice. Like I said before, an arranged marriage was not for me, but the longing in the eyes of my mother and the guilt of not having taken charge of this aspect of my life made me blurt out that dangerous word, 'okay'. The next thing I remember is being on a flight en route to a first-hand experience of something that seems unimaginable today and, frankly, quite unnecessary.

My memories are blurry, maybe conveniently forgotten, but I do remember flashes of being toured around this very wealthy yet sweet family's business estate and properties. After a build-up to the main event of the itinerary, I got to meet the young lady only later in the afternoon, long after having exhausted myself with thoughts oscillating between the purposelessness of this trip and anger towards my parents. Nevertheless, I attempted to maintain a positive attitude, one of trying something completely out of the box for me and, even more so, tried to do what was expected of me as a dutiful son. Also, it was quite clear to me by then that there was no way out of this fortress till I had completed the necessary steps and fulfilled all obligations. Yes, this was supposed to be a trip for me and my future, but it felt more like I was obliging a number of people: my family, the family in front of me and, above all, destiny.

The lady in question was rather quiet, agreeable and very well-mannered. But I couldn't see the remotest possibility of a future together for us, and that's not because I was there for the rendezvous only because I felt obliged. Very few words were spoken between us and I realized that there were glaring differences between our personalities and backgrounds. Her family, especially her father, was quick to note this sense of cultural shock and disappointment in my eyes, and made sincere efforts to convince me that there had been extremely successful marriages between strikingly different people who'd worked to make a life together worthwhile. Don't get me wrong here: I'm not judging this lady at all. Her quietness needn't have meant that she was unintelligent or boring. Also, her willingness to make a success of this effort between our families wasn't necessarily an indication of some sort of desperation. Her parents seemed sweet, even though I wasn't spared a second and then a third round of property tours and financial history. I too take time to warm up to strangers and have difficulty deciding whether I'm more an introvert or an extrovert. But the most important reality of this whole exercise was that something didn't click. In fact, nothing clicked, and I was delighted to be back on my seat on the return flight, the dutiful son, with a strong sense of accomplishment. The next thing I remember is that I was back home, in my bed the same night and back to my comfort zone. Phew!

Besides my own realization of the passage of time and my family's impatience, another very important sensation had begun to emerge. I was getting drawn to small children and would often stop to watch them play in parks and other recreational areas. I can vividly recall watching and discussing the cuteness of young kids with their parents in the swimming pool that overlooked my regular gym, and in a subtle way, would express a desire to have one of my own. These instances would lead to almost nothing. I'd invariably always fall back on my work, which was quite hectic at that time. My work kept me busy, challenged, fulfilled and, most importantly, gave me the courage to tell myself, 'Where's the time to plan a family and have kids?' Nevertheless, the fact that I was also getting attached to my pet dog Poshto, a black Pomeranian, and had begun nurturing him like a child at home, proved one thing for sure. I had that 'something' growing inside of me, a prerequisite for any good parent: something natural, pure and unique to every individual. Undoubtedly, I was developing a strong paternal instinct.

Life had its share of ups and downs, but I was happy with what was being thrown at me, at least as far as my career as an actor was concerned. By that time in 2012, I had several hit movies to my credit and a special franchise had just released its second instalment, *Kyaa Super Kool Hain Hum*, to strong box-office collections. Yet, I wanted more. I wanted to capitalize on this recent success as a stepping stone to greater heights, and then repeat the magic that came with my debut film, *Mujhe Kucch Kehna Hai*, a solo hero box-office superhit. The unpredictability of my line of work and the sometimes cruel hand of fate, or karma, if you wish to call it that, can delay the outcome of passionate zeal, no matter how hard you persevere or how patiently you hold on. Still, I was grateful to be busy, popular and always fortunate enough to get another chance just when I needed it. To get the right perspective on life and the nature of things, I'd also spend time relaxing with friends, exercising and catching up on any and every film at the nearby cinemas.

That year I revisited my college town, Ann Arbor, after a gap of more than three years. I had been back several times since graduating in 1998. These trips would help me destress and disconnect from the madness of Mumbai and its film world. This time, too, I was looking forward to doing the same, especially before new film assignments were slated to begin. Besides visiting my favourite eateries, like Backroom Pizza Slice Corner and China Gate, I reconnected with old friends and associates from my years as a student. My days were filled with fun and frolic, and conversations with senior colleagues brought new insights and perspectives into the idea of parenting. An old confidante of mine suggested I research a fertility centre in one of the southern US states, Colorado, I think, that had successfully helped single men and women start families of their own outside of marriage. She was talking about the idea of becoming a parent through in vitro fertilization (IVF) and surrogacy, in case I wasn't cut out for marriage at all. At first, I was excited about the idea and thought that this might just turn out to be a viable option for someone like me. But every time I thought about actually researching this possibility and then enquiring further about the legalities for an Indian citizen, it felt absurd, to say the least. But hey, why not investigate the possibility of some such hospital back home in India?

However, the thought of even starting an online search enquiry about fertility centres anywhere in the world would turn into an agonizing dilemma. I would shut myself off from the audacity of venturing into a territory entirely unknown to me. Was it anxiety? Did I feel like all this would lead to nothing? Did I not want it badly enough? Or did I really want to wait for a love marriage to happen? Frankly, I don't have the answers to what I was thinking and feeling then. All I remember is being proud that I had at least started talking about and considering the idea of having a family. At that point, that was more than enough for me. I was on a self-planned vacation in Michigan, without any of the usual suspects from my Mumbai life, and that was good enough for me to unwind and go down memory lane.

Like all good things, even good vacations must come to an end. After very long, I felt like I had really made the most of a travel plan and done everything in just two weeks. The return to the grind of everyday life has its moments of discomfort amid adjustment and, sometimes, even a little bit of despair. But this time, something happened that made me feel like I was being made to pay a price for a break that gave me more than I had bargained for. I'm not talking about the crushing jetlag caused by an over twenty-hour non-stop flight, nor had I lost any of the suitcases that contained my indulgences in athletic wear and toiletries. My plight had more to do with what I saw when I entered my bedroom, tired and exhausted, while still figuring out the time zone I was in. The furniture in my room had been rearranged and the décor looked unrecognizable. I could see sunflowers hanging out of vases on a shelf on which I had previously arranged picture frames that matched the colour contrasts in the rest of the room. I earlier lived in a room with minimalistic decor. But what stood in front of me was a far cry from that, and there was more to come. The cabinet of shelves which stored my DVD collection, mostly my own previous films, now looked like it had been turned upside down. It became clear to me that someone had presided over a partial overhaul of my personal living space, my bedroom. For someone who takes a certain pride in being very organized, to the point of being obsessive-compulsive about the minutest of things, what welcomed me in my bedroom that night left me with no option but to create a furore. I felt aghast, betrayed and consumed with anger and rage.

When I raised hell, I discovered that my mother had done the deed on the advice of a feng shui expert whom she consulted. Apparently, they felt that my room needed changes that would help make me look on the brighter side of life, marriage, particularly, and perhaps take the plunge soon. 'Oh, so that is why I see sunflowers? To make me happier? So who thinks I'm not happy and have a negative view towards life and marriage?' Thoughts like these made me even more agitated. The fact is that I do believe in the institution of marriage and have never expressed a contrary opinion. Owing to an independent lifestyle and personality as an adult, it might not have seemed like an eventuality to me then, and it doesn't now. But that doesn't mean I'm blind to the fact that billions have found love, strength, hope and true happiness through marriage and its challenges. Anyway, that whole debate is a little besides the point. Obviously, I reprimanded my mother quite harshly for doing the unthinkable. We didn't speak for almost a month after that. This disaster had to have some resolution. I took solace in learning that no one from the family, even guided by their best intentions, would invade my personal space again.

The next few months in 2013 were challenging professionally, as a return to work often is after a blissful vacation. I had three projects that had to be worked on back-to-back, at times almost simultaneously. They included a TV comedy show as a judge, the fairly successful gangster drama called *Shootout at Wadala* and a slightly offbeat slice-of-life film called *Bajatey Raho*. Each of these projects was challenging for the focus and commitment that was required of me, and also in terms of handling the different teams of professionals on each set. I recall a pressing time when I had to be on two different shooting sets on the same day and during the same period. *Shootout at Wadala* had a final song sequence, '*Aala Re Aala*', that had to be filmed throughout the day, and the comedy show had its episode shoot after 12 p.m. Fortunately, they both happened to be in Film City and very close to one another. Somehow, I managed to convince Sanjay Gupta, the producer and director of the film, to allow me to leave around noon, after the completion of my work on the song. I had a supporting role in this dance sequence and Sanjay sir agreed to alter the shot division—the line-up of shots, to put it simply— to accommodate my presence in the first half of the day's schedule. I was planning to finish the film shoot and reach the sets of the TV show next door in time, with a delay of not more than an hour, which in such situations is par for the course. Perfect!

No prizes for guessing how that day unfolded for me. The song shoot didn't start filming on time, like it always happens on the sets of an extravagant dance sequence. I landed up shooting just two major shots by the time it was noon and had to settle for just that, even after stretching myself for longer than I possibly could. Though my contribution to this song was never big, it was painful to sacrifice a more substantial presence in a potential Bollywood-style chartbuster on top of the embarrassment of having to tell a senior director in the middle of his shoot, 'Sir, I have to leave.' To make matters worse, I reached the set of the other work commitment, only to be told upon my arrival that I had to start getting ready immediately as they had been delayed because of me and needed to catch up on lost time. Exhausted, I had no choice but to accept the unexpected turn of events and move on with my day, hoping to find some meaning and method to this madness. *C'est la vie!*

During such months, when work would be hectic and mentally exhausting too, it always took precedence over other areas of my life, especially my concerns about entering my late thirties with no plan for starting a family. The year 2013, like the year before it, was also when my hard work and perseverance paid off in gratifying results. *Shootout at Wadala* released to a good response in May and though there was much to debate in the varying degrees of success it received in different parts of India, it eventually settled into a paying proposal for one and all. The real icing on the cake was the critical acclaim I received for my performance as a gangster who has a heart of gold and loyalty like none other. That also helped me remain undefeated by the lukewarm box-office response to *Bajatey*

Raho, a film that went largely unnoticed when it released in July that year.

In the period that followed, I had time to ponder over my personal life choices—marriage, children and everything else under the sun that needed attention. I chose to watch television instead and got hooked to a highly popular reality show where people of varying temperaments and issues are made to live together and are captured on camera. Unabashedly voyeuristic, the show relies on this unnatural setting wherein celebrities with controversial backgrounds and fiery personalities instigate one another and create the famous Bollywood-style drama which now seems more real than ever. I think, subconsciously, this worked for me in more ways than just entertainment. I had a feeling that I was waking up to, almost taking refuge in, the fact that there are all kinds of people in this world. Everyone is different, imperfect, and finding solutions to problems they never started. People fight, sometimes a lot, get confused, crumble under pressure, overreact and mostly do things very differently from the societal norms that rule our sense of what's appropriate and what's not. Yes, that's the part I believe resonated with me and my dilemma about being single, even as I was entering my late thirties. This show made me feel less stressed, more accepting of my life story and even willing to go with the flow though, really, there appeared to be no commonality between my journey thus far and the journeys of these contestants. I guess it's true that, sometimes, the most unconventional, uncanny things can help us let our hair down and even get a better perspective on our lives.

The year 2013 gave me much to be grateful for. Besides decent success at the box office, I also enjoyed playing judge for the first time on a television comedy show and, finally, as mentioned above, I'd found a reality show to entertain myself at dinner time, like a stress buster that helped me tide over the daily grind. The highlight of the year, though, was a completely fresh professional development that could add a new dimension to my career, as well as open up avenues that hadn't been explored before. Between acting assignments, I had been working with a friend on selecting a good script to produce a film together. We had zeroed in on the Tamil blockbuster film *Muni 2: Kanchana* (2011) as the story that we wanted to remake in Hindi for Bollywood audiences. In August of that year, we finally managed to secure the remake rights of this horror-comedy. In the meantime, the leading man we had in mind had also agreed to headline the cast of the Hindi version. Things were falling into place in this area and something that started as an idea was now materializing into a dream project. It was a bold step for me, but venturing into film production much ahead of my contemporaries could add another feather to my cap. As a film actor, things could've moved faster, but with so much else going on and now on the threshold of becoming a mainstream Hindi film producer, I felt obliged to pat myself on the back and say, 'Everything is fine.'

I was able to hold on to this positivity even at the start of 2014. But another reality was also catching up and that was the fact that, somewhere, my acting career lacked momentum. Film offers were aplenty, though none exciting enough to give my heart and soul to. In the past, during such low phases, I admit I'd feel a bit weighed down and mildly depressed too. But this time, I found the strength to introspect and accept that such phases are normal in the life of any actor—I was definitely no exception. I had patience, yet felt spurred on to take stock of all that was not working out and make necessary amends. Timing is everything in this profession, but in terms of what I was doing, what could be going wrong? Something told me I needed to be audacious enough to get out of my comfort zone, like I did when venturing into film production. Without wasting time, I began redirecting fresh energy into strategizing for my career and started reaching out to directors I wanted to work with, especially those I hadn't worked with previously. Maybe some industry folks misunderstood my slightly introverted nature as one that lacked the necessary fire or dynamism, or maybe they thought I didn't want to work with people I wasn't accustomed to. In any case, I felt that this false perception needed to change.

At the cost of sounding eager and needy, I admit I also made efforts to be socially visible and network more often. For this, I had to shed my childhood inhibitions and worry about being seen and perceived incorrectly, and needed to operate by the old Bollywood mantra: *Jo dikhta hai woh bikta hai*. I was never excited by the idea of dressing up to attend a red-carpet event or even a late-night movie premiere of the next blockbuster. Honestly, I couldn't be bothered. But as I was beginning a professional makeover of sorts, for the next couple of months, I went all out and attended every important social event that I was invited to. I even ended up going to a very prestigious award function without an invitation. For many years, they had been relentlessly pursuing me to attend and, by now, having given up on me, had not bothered to even send me a text message. For this one, I also had company in a senior actress who wanted to come along, perform the niceties and make her presence felt, just like me. To my surprise, I stayed much longer than I had expected to and enjoyed the experience as well. Good for me, I thought.

So, did the trick work? I mean, was the effort of transforming my personal relations as a movie star an exercise in futility or did the strategy pay off? Well, it definitely gave me a sense of belonging to the film fraternity, greater visibility in the media and, strangely, even work satisfaction, though I was mostly only socializing. My readers might find this strange, for everyone thinks that actors born to actors have it together at all times and needn't worry about waiting for roles on merit; we are supposed to have inherited a bed of roses which includes movie assignments through connections. The fact is, no matter who you are, you are all alone in your struggles and only as good as your last film, and, in my case, sometimes even that didn't matter. Yet, I always believed in working hard, in God and in creating good causes for sorting out my work karma. But did exciting movie offers come by? Yes and no. I did sign two films in that period, one called *Mastizaade* and the other, the third instalment of the *Kya Kool Hain Hum* franchise, called *Kya Kool Hain Hum 3*. But were these a result of meeting directors from my wish list or the media blitzkrieg following 'handsome' appearances? Maybe, I can't say. Most of the star producers and directors I met had words of wisdom to share and expressed a desire to collaborate 'at the right time'. Some of those whom I tried to connect with never responded, while others sent feelers that I felt were a desire to be chased for a chance to meet with them. It does take all sorts of narcissistic people, too, to make up this world, and Bollywood is no exception. Nevertheless, it's also true that in Bollywood, like in every industry, hard work does pay off. One small, brave step can lead to another, creating a chain reaction that can bring about positive results.

The flip side to the coin was that both the films I had signed were adult comedies in the genre of funny films like *American Pie* and *Meet the Fockers*. Was I making a mistake in agreeing to work on two films of the same genre, and that too adult comedies? I liked the humour in both. The zone had worked for me before and now also gave me the opportunity to get that major commercial success which would thrust my career back into the right gear. As the saying goes, 'Great things never came from comfort zones.'

With two promising acting assignments and a mammoth production venture under my belt, the first quarter of 2014 proved a rocking start to the year. Having evolved into a more media-savvy actor, my next mantra was working towards the real challenge of preparing for these two films. *Mastizaade*, the first to begin pre-production, required me to work on myself for a special pole-dancing sequence in the comedy. Yes, you read that correctly. A pole-dancing sequence with both the heroes of the film, and the director wanted it to look authentic. Holy moly! Something needed to change, for sure, and I mean drastically. I had to lose the extra adipose gained in all the partying and socializing in the months leading up to this. Therefore, after considerable research, I moved into a new form of fitness training called HIIT or high-intensity interval training, with an instructor who was demanding, to say the least. In addition to high levels of strength and endurance, I understood that this gruelling, intense workout regime also needed to be completed within a short time frame, a feat that required mental strength above everything else. Thankfully, the end result was like a gift of rejuvenation, pure bliss, and I felt charged enough to take on the world. My weight loss was instant and I felt lighter than ever in a matter of just a few days. The dreaded pole-dancing sequence now didn't seem like it would be such a nightmare. With new films, new marketing vigour and a new movement coach, my acting career felt promising all over again. Life was good!

In the discussion about the twists and turns to my career in this chapter, I seem to have lost track of the family-planning aspect and the other concerns that I had to endure, which is how it is in life. I was so engrossed with my work life in those months of 2013 and 2014 that I took the other personal issues very lightly, completely for granted. Little did I know that in chasing my dreams as an actor, I was also coming closer to figuring out what was in store for me in the other real dilemmas of my life. The maze had really only begun.

Divine Intervention

An actor's life is such that when things in one area start to fall in place, it's inevitable that something somewhere else will bring fresh challenges. Yes, this is life too, but the regularity with which it hits you in our profession almost feels like some external power is holding you accountable for your success. Which is why we are always anxious, even in good times, not knowing where the next curveball is coming from. The situation I'm referring to is the first major setback of 2014, a pressing issue in the *Kanchana* remake. A couple of leading members of the film's cast expressed their inability to be a part of the film, owing to a certain disconnect with their characters and roles in the script. They were straightforward about it and, in a dignified manner, encouraged us to move forward without them. Initially, this change of heart and their departure felt like a bolt from the blue, but soon we found the gumption to take it in our stride as part of the process of filmmaking. I'm an actor too, and I understand the disagreements that all actors have as far as their choice of roles and scripts are concerned. This time I was on the other side, and it dawned upon me that I had to toughen up to the realities of this new world of film production. Without wasting time, my co-producer and I began working towards suitable and equally exciting replacements for these actors. We had no choice but to believe—to believe that whatever happens, happens for the best. Even in showbiz.

Mastizaade, on the other hand, started on a fruitful note and, despite some bumps along the way, turned out to be a happy shooting experience. Yes, even the pole-dancing sequence was shot well and I looked fit enough to save myself any embarrassment. Before we knew it the shooting was over, right in time to ring in the year-end celebrations. Even *Kyaa Kool Hain Hum 3*, shot in early 2015, was a blast right from the word go. It was a home production produced by my sister Ekta and I was working with friends like Aftab Shivdasani, my co-star in the film, and a young crew of new talent that had the passion and hunger to make a success of this film. Both these projects had adult humour which, if not handled correctly, could backfire and even cause a backlash for the film. We thought we understood that and went ahead with full gusto and the ambition to bring the house down in the cinemas, never mind the risqué humour. This is where I think we lost sight of the fact that, maybe, we were going overboard. Undoubtedly the scripts were funny, but the writers, under pressure to raise the bar and outdo the previous comedies of this genre, had tried to make the humour bolder than had ever been seen in Hindi cinema. It turned out to be a colossal mistake.

In May 2015, while filming a scene for the last schedule of *Kyaa Kool Hain Hum 3*, I got the news that *Mastizaade* had been denied a censor certificate. Until then I had heard of films being rated A, 'adults only', or being granted a certificate for a lower-age category, like 'UA' or 'U', subject to a few or no deletions from the film. This was the norm within the Indian rating system. An outright denial of certification meant nothing short of a disaster. Today, I understand the reasons behind what happened, but back then, my dismay only deepened as I began ruminating about what lay ahead for the movie. Also, I had to focus on my shoot that day for a film that had similar content and might have to face a similar struggle. To top it all, obviously, this news leaked and social media was abuzz with headlines that stated, '*Mastizaade* banned!' The only silver lining to this mess was an unexpected break of a few days before we wrapped up the last schedule of *Kyaa Kool* . . . With my first movie production already in a crisis and dwindling fortunes for the two hard-earned acting projects, I felt like I had no option but to seek some divine intervention.

I'm usually a passively religious person, but it has been a tradition for me to visit the Lord Balaji temple in

Tirupati at least once each year. At the cost of sounding superstitious, I have to admit I do believe in its power and have felt less stressed after visiting the shrine on the eve of any film's release. This time, though, the story was a little different. I was going to pray for a film to, first, have a fair chance to even get a cinematic release. The film in question, *Mastizaade*, had to secure a censor certificate, or else the efforts and hopes of everyone associated with it would go down the drain. I felt confident that when all else fails, God, especially Lord Balaji, has the answers.

The journey to Tirupati and then further up the mountain to the temple town of Tirumala has always been an arduous task. The Chennai airport was the only one in the vicinity, so travellers from Mumbai had to fly there and then drive for endless hours to the temple town. Well, all that has changed over the years, mercifully, for people like me who don't like travelling too much. At the time of the *Mastizaade* censorship crisis, direct flights from Mumbai to Tirupati via Hyderabad had begun operating.

I remember getting in the plane excitedly and taking my seat in the front row of the early morning flight. Just then, I noticed that the seat next to me was occupied by well-known film director Prakash Jha, famous for Hindi heartland realistic dramas like *Gangaajal* and *Raajneeti*, among many. Having interacted with him briefly on a few occasions in the past, I should have rejoiced at the idea of having such a companion on the flight. However, given his stature and seniority within the film industry, I initially felt awkward making conversation. Of course, this had a lot to do with my own shyness. I had to remind myself to be assertive and recognize the situation as an opportunity, to present myself as an actor who was seeking good work. Here, I must make an honest admission. No matter how much actors from my generation present themselves as being detached and too cool to think about films beyond the sets, the fact is that we all, or at least most of us, are obsessed with our careers and the chance for growth and success. Likewise, I was no different. Not anymore, at least.

Within no time, we were discussing movies, politics and our reasons for this trip. If I remember correctly, Mr Jha was visiting the shrine before he began the marathon shooting schedule of his next, *Jai Gangaajal*, the sequel to *Gangaajal* (2003). He too was on a day trip, though we had different flights back to Mumbai the next afternoon. We exchanged numbers before deplaning at Tirupati airport and promised to try and connect even during this short trip.

My preference has been to conduct the pilgrimage in the traditional style, so I've mostly woken up at 4 a.m. and walked up the hill to the main shrine in Tirumala. This time, too, instead of taking the car, I was eager to climb those many thousand steps. This challenging route usually takes me about two hours, a personal record of sorts, and despite the exhausting exercise, makes me feel like a true devotee ready for his 6 a.m. rendezvous with God. As always, darshan with Lord Balaji took me another two hours and I was back in my hotel room by around 8.30, hoping to relax for some time before returning to Mumbai. If memory serves me correctly, just as I was about to fall into deep sleep, I was woken up by frantic calls and messages from the travel agent in Mumbai. Unfortunately, my flight had been cancelled and though there were alternative flights, they were mostly for the next day or the day after that. That's also what I don't like about travelling: you never know when your plans go haywire. The only way to get to Mumbai the same day was to drive to Chennai airport and take an evening flight back. I don't remember exactly what was going on that day but, coincidentally, Mr Jha also had the same issue with his flight and called me, enquiring about a solution to this flight problem. After some deliberation, it was decided that we would take the same car to Chennai together and take an evening flight back to Mumbai. That way, the over-three-hour drive wouldn't feel as long, especially since we had no choice but to make the most of this unusual and unexpected turn of events. Truly, man proposes, God disposes.

It had been ages since I had taken the rocky ride between Chennai and Tirupati, but this time, the roads were smooth and the drive back felt breezy. That might also have been due to the fact that the difference in seniority between Mr Jha and me didn't seem like too much of a roadblock. I guess that's what a minor crisis can do. It can bring people closer and unite them towards a common goal or purpose. There was also much to talk about. Gradually, the conversation veered towards my career and he asked why, unlike many other actors, I wasn't seen much in the media. It was both flattering and a bit unnerving when he opined that despite my being part of many blockbuster movies, actors with a lesser repertoire to boast of were grabbing far more headlines thanks to their relationships and controversies. I explained to him that most of my successes had been as part of an ensemble cast and not as a solo hero, leaving me less than confident about shouting victory from the rooftops. It was also just not my personality to ask for attention, even in the very commercial movie business where any form of publicity, even negative publicity, can be fruitful. I'd much rather let my work do the talking. Usually, such conversations about my relationship with the limelight of Bollywood would make me a bit uncomfortable, since a part of me felt that I needed to really blend in with most other actors and not stand out so differently. However, Prakash ji seemed to have a different take on it all.

Rather than patronizing me and advising me to change myself in some way, he said, 'Tusshar, you're an actor who's also clued in to worldly matters like politics, unlike many others who don't know what's going on in the country outside of films. Obviously, you're not the type who would be comfortable flaunting every move to the paparazzi, neither would you manipulate the media to carry details about your personal life.' His analysis of my personality type and my career choices was interesting. Even though I wasn't yet ready to celebrate my shortcomings in carrying myself like a film star as being related to personal depth and intelligence, these observations definitely had a positive impact on my self-esteem. A serious director had just made me recognize my true persona as an actor, hopefully heralding a shift from the self-doubt I carried within, of being some sort of an 'Alice' in Bollywood land.

As we spoke about actors, media, relationships, etc., he wondered what I had in mind for myself regarding marriage and family. After years of dodging this question in embarrassing conversations, by then I had an honest confession for anyone who asked. 'Sir, I'm going with the flow; I don't know about the future. I guess I'll know I'm ready to take the plunge when I find the right life partner to settle down with. Until then, I'm absolutely fine and occupied, too, being single.' Refreshingly, he didn't retort with the usual, 'Tusshar, get married now. It's time to settle down and find a life partner for yourself!' As a single parent himself, and having seen more life than most other marriage propagandists within our families and social circles, he understood the situation of not having the right answer to this question. However, like the part of me that was concerned about the need to have kids at the right age, he spoke about another alternative to marriage. Yes, single parenthood and not necessarily adoption. Phew!

Deep down, I must've heaved a major sigh of relief to know that there was someone, a single parent with experience, wishing to help me with some major life decisions. As I mentioned earlier, I had been informed about certain procedures before as well. This time, the icing on the cake was the fact that Mr Jha was from my fraternity and my city, Mumbai, too. I was eagerly trying to get more information. 'Has anyone done something like this outside of marriage, in a conservative society like India?' I asked. As the conversation continued, I knew something felt right, that some divine intervention was already beginning to manifest itself.

Mr Jha enlightened me about the possibility of IVF and surrogacy in Mumbai, and that there were people, single men and women both, who had successfully crossed that bridge into parenthood. He told me about Mrs Ruprani Parikh, a friend of his who had helped her single daughter, Rutu Parikh, take the plunge and become the mother of a baby girl simply using technology and, above all, by making up her mind. As difficult as it is to believe, Mr Jha dialled Ruprani from the car the very next moment and I had an insightful conversation with her about what could be in store for me. She was reassuring, to say the least, with a confident tone that exuded warmth and a willingness to help. 'Don't worry, beta, it's all possible, I'll explain the entire procedure to you once you're back. You just have to make up your mind and I'll take you to the doctor who will guide you with what needs to be done,' she told me. She asked me to meet her as soon as I was back and ready, and also offered to introduce me to her daughter Rutu, as well as see her grandchild Ahilya, who was then a year old.

I can say with certainty today that, at that point, somewhere deep down, I had already made up my mind to do what they were suggesting to me. Of course, a zillion emotions still clouded my thinking and I needed some time. Those emotions included primarily anxiety over several questions that sprung up, one among them being, 'What about life after becoming a single parent? Is a fulfilling life even feasible? One has to be happy first to be able to devote his life to the happiness of another, right?' To this, Prakash ji spoke about his own experience adopting a girl child and bringing her up all by himself. I recall him speaking about taking his baby to his film and television shoots and his memories of multitasking, feeding the baby in between the shots.

I was amazed. His confidence spoke of how happy he had been with his choice, despite the inevitable challenges. Also, there was a life lesson in all of this: that if you genuinely want something, from the depths of your heart, you can definitely make it happen. Like Mrs Parikh, he too offered to introduce me to his grown-up, teenaged daughter. I couldn't believe this had all played out as a result of some flight cancellations. It must have been destiny, which usually comes knocking on one's door in inexplicable ways. Well, at least that's what I told myself.

Both Mr Jha and Mrs Parikh told me to think hard before making a decision, and they were right. Despite all the positivity, excitement and constructive advice, I was aware that there were bound to be several more doubts and fears that could come up, especially in such a brilliant yet bold opportunity. The beauty of it all was the fact that, finally, I had come to a point where I felt energized enough to think seriously about the

WITH MR PRAKASH JHA DURING THE FLIGHT FROM CHENNAI TO MUMBAI AFTER A RIGOROUS JOURNEY OF TWISTS AND TURNS TO LORD BALAJI!

challenges that lay ahead and work on my anxieties before making any informed decision.

Before we knew it, we were at the airport lounge in Chennai, catching up on the news, hoping our flight wouldn't get delayed yet again. I have no memory of the flight back, though, probably owing to exhaustion and a desperation to get back home after a tiring journey.

Mumbai, with its glitter and its grime, has a way of bringing you back to your realities, no matter where you come from. I got back into my routine, inching towards the final schedule of *Kyaa Kool Hain Hum 3* and awaiting any further development with this disaster called *Mastizaade*. However, amid all this, there was one voice that kept playing at the back of my mind, and it had nothing to do with films, friends or my regular routine. All I could sense and hear was, 'Thank you God, thank you Balaji.'

The shooting of *Kyaa Kool Hain Hum 3* was completed on schedule—a film I'll never forget for the sheer pleasure of working with friends and also the calmness of the others associated with it. Thereafter, I had the time to think about the whole discussion with Mr Jha and, of course, the way ahead. Here, I must admit that I didn't have the gumption to speak to Mrs Parikh immediately. Naturally, a lot seemed to be going on that was holding me back.

As a mildly shy person, I've always hesitated playing to the gallery, even when it's required in situations that are legitimized by the demands of my profession. It's always that fear of 'too much' of anything, especially when something is public, that keeps me holding back. Sometimes I've miscalculated and wished I'd gone the whole hog, like in the case of my media savviness. Often, I've also been better off not indulging myself, and have even had the last laugh because of my belief that less is more. However, here, the story was very different. I was confronted with a choice that could change my life in ways that were absolutely unforeseeable in conventional circumstances. I won't be lying if I said that I was beginning to feel a bit abnormal, too, for thinking so unconventionally. Jokes apart, with my personal life under constant public and media scrutiny anyway, this bold decision would necessitate a public announcement at some point. My biological child, without a marriage, would have to be brought into this world with honesty and dignity. Getting to the point, such an announcement had the potential of making even 'too much' seem like an understatement. Was I ready for that?

It's one thing to have clarity of thought and to not worry about what others think. But here, we were not talking about shedding inhibitions or getting out of one's comfort zone. This was about shaking, almost breaking, the sociocultural fabric of a society, one that prides itself on traditions like marriage, family and everything else that comes with it. So what were my real apprehensions?

What is going to be everyone's reaction to my choice of family life? Will I wake up to newspaper headlines trying to decode the reasons for such an audacity, speculation about my personal life and, above all, my child? Like with Michael Jackson, will people think there is something wrong with me? Will I be ostracized by the cinema viewing public and is this going to be doomsday as far as my career is concerned? And in the event that the general public is okay with my choice of family life, will this new role of an unconventional father limit my choice of roles within the film fraternity? Yes, these were all very scary thoughts, but before I say more, I'd like to state one thing for sure. I wasn't being a coward, not in the least.

In my fifteen years as an actor, I had braved many storms of wrongful publicity, misquoting by the print media and had even withstood a couple of glaring wardrobe malfunctions that haven't been forgotten. During one dance performance on stage, I was to pull my trousers down, but I pulled my underwear down along with them, inadvertently putting my booty on full display for a few seconds. I still suffer some embarrassment on account of that even today, but I had the guts to put that behind me in the spirit of it all being part of an actor's life. But here, I was faced with a choice that surpassed the very meaning of breaking norms and being daring, and there was no precedent in my professional world to gauge what might be the repercussions. Also, if you're thinking that all I cared about was a potential tsunami in the media and a possible catastrophe in my career, you're wrong. There was more to come.

The other big issue concerned my immediate family, and obviously their views and happiness. As an adult nearing his forties, I had the confidence to not let my family decide what was best for me, particularly as far as marriage and career were concerned. Here, I must give them credit, too, for letting me have my independence and not pressuring me to do anything. Still, given the fact that they were waiting for some good news from my side, I wondered what their state of mind would be in the event that I decided to become a 'bachelor dad'. Of course, any plans of organizing a grand wedding ceremony (or ceremonies) would be negated. The Indian parents' dream of nurturing a typical joint family with grandchildren et al. would also need major readjustment. Above all, what were their views about my preparedness and maturity for this new phase of my life, especially without a life partner? My mother had witnessed my paternal instincts in nurturing Poshto, my pet dog, for years now. She felt I was ready for fatherhood and had expressed a burning desire to enjoy it with me. But it's one thing to believe in one's readiness to father a child, it's quite another to think one can do it all by oneself. Basically, a part of me was crying out for reassurance. I needed their encouragement and faith in my extraordinary decision, so that it felt right and not like grave injustice to both the child and me.

This brings me to the most important, and probably the only really important, aspect of the entire rigmarole: my child and I. Amid the avalanche of concerns and apprehensions regarding what the public might think, the potential media backlash and the wishes of my family, I realized I was forgetting to ask me, myself, what *I* thought of it all. To come in touch with the truth that existed within me. Simply, did I also think that there was something abnormal in pursuing assisted reproductive procedures to become a father? Or that the whole idea was more like a celebrity whim or fancy that lacked seriousness or the emotional gravitas associated with becoming a parent? Well, the answer, obviously, was a big 'no'.

I was an adult who, despite believing in marriage and family ties, never ended up tying the knot. Here, not that it really matters, it nevertheless must be stated that I don't belong to a dysfunctional family. I have grown up witnessing a highly successful Bollywood marriage, that of my parents, that has withstood the test of time and the vagaries of showbiz. In my case, though, at times the relationship wasn't worth sacrificing my peace of mind for, while, at other times, either trust or just chemistry was missing. If, after all these years, being single has felt reasonably okay and a far more fulfilling experience than a marriage that would be more in keeping with the norms of family and society, then so be it. Who knows, I still might get married someday. Never say never, right? In addition, as a single man, why can't I have a child of my own? There seems to be an unwritten rule for single individuals wanting to become fathers and mothers, that dictates adoption as the obvious choice over everything else. Yes, I'm not denying adoption is great and can even be a lifesaver for a lost soul, but I wanted to do it my way, to have my own, biological child. In that case, who decides what's moral and what's not? As far as I know, eventually, what matters is the intention behind bringing a life into this world. If the answer to that is 'pure love', then any other argument just does not hold water. Don't billions of married couples choose to have their own kids? Then why couldn't I?

This kind of introspection lightened my feeling of inadequacy. Suddenly, what society or the media would think or have in store for me was not a major concern. I understood the importance of having a dialogue with my own conscience and also learnt that what really mattered, and should matter, to anyone is the honesty in leading a life of integrity. Once that is assured, other voices lose power and feel like nothing more than pure humbug. Very well, then.

We all know that actors in every part of the world have done crazy things in their personal lives and that too without any fear of the repercussions as far as their public image is concerned. The beauty of it all has been the fact that loving fans and moviegoers have accepted these idiosyncrasies as part of being human and a part of their idols' personal lives. Sometimes, evidently, the crazier and wilder it gets, the greater is the aura of the movie star. On the other hand, I was a relatively unassuming actor, leading a simple life and with a simple desire to father a child. If that was the case, why would the audience think any differently? Also, given the fact that there were millions of unmarried individuals stuck in the belief that they had no choice but to live alone, this bold step of mine had the pathbreaking potential to show many the way to light at the end of the tunnel. And what did my personal choice of parenting have anything to do with the kind of roles that would be offered to me in my line of work? So then, why worry about being seen as unheroic and deviant, and hence marginalized by my fraternity?

In a nutshell, my feelings of self-doubt and unrest were crystallizing into an idea that as long as my conscience was clear, I needn't worry about being answerable to the external world. But there was one person I would always be most answerable to, all my life: my child. My child's upbringing, wellness and happiness was my responsibility; therefore I had to face the reality that, despite the joys, parenting under any circumstances was not a cakewalk. So, honestly, was I cut out for the job of taking up this huge responsibility? Would I be able to pull off this challenge and do justice to my child as a bachelor dad? Did I have it in me to be the loving, nurturing, sacrificing, understanding father who was available when he was needed and who could be all these things at the same time, even when it seemed impossible? Well, I had no clue about the answers to so many of these questions. It would've been preposterous of me to figure out a barometer to judge myself and then decide my eligibility. I understood that life didn't work that way for anyone and had no place for mathematics, especially in the realm of personal life decisions. However, from the bottom of my heart, I knew that I had enough love in me to devote a large part of my existence to the well-being of my child and, for that, I was willing to find the best version of myself on the good days as well as the bad. I might not turn out to be perfect, but I had what it took to work around every challenge and do my best. Somewhere, I got my answer.

By then I had almost made up my mind to call Mrs Ruprani Parikh for a meeting and move ahead with my little master plan. Somewhere along the way, and I really don't know why, I didn't feel the need to consult my parents either. From fearing the worst professionally to needing family support, I finally came to a point where this decision became entirely mine. The conflicts were mine and the resolutions had to be mine too. I felt confident, even though there was an emerging anticipation and nervous energy that brought to light some other, very important considerations. One of them came up in a conversation with a tarot card reader way back in 2013. At my birthday dinner that year, around the time I had barely started flirting with this idea, some of my friends and I had asked her whether single parenting through assisted reproductive procedures was a feasible option. I remember giving examples of many international celebrities who, having taken the plunge, completed their lives without marriage. At first she just stared at us, expressionless. Then, almost as if we ought to have known, she brought up the issue of bullying and name-calling that children of single parents could be subjected to in school. To my disappointment, she had a point. Children, under the garb of being curious, can be quite insensitive and cause their peers great anxiety. A child is victimized, suffers adverse psychological consequences and can sometimes also get scarred for life.

I argued that today's schools, especially those with an international curriculum and mindset, don't encourage an atmosphere conducive to such situations and behaviour. Also, that a new-age school would provide, besides an emotionally secure environment, appropriate counselling in the event that a child was targeted in such a way. I also remember the lady not reacting to my argument, almost as if it seemed like an unrealistic illusion to her. Anyway, that conversation didn't last very long but, strangely, came back to my mind during my own decision-making process later.

Another possibility that reared its ugly head was that of a situation in which the child grows up and asks me the truth about his/her mother. Before dwelling any further on it, thankfully, I realized that overthinking the entire matter would open up a Pandora's box and only add to more confusion. I was aware that I had the guidance and experience of beautiful people like Mr Prakash Jha and Mrs Parikh to rely on. It was only the beginning of my life-changing process, so if the excitement was high, it's understandable that the nervousness would be much greater. Above all, there was enough time to understand and resolve any unforeseen dilemmas, therefore, I felt positive that I'd reached a point where there was no looking back, at least for the time being. So, for any further doubts, misgivings and madness that cried for attention and threatened to make me hyper, I just whispered to myself, 'Will cross that bridge when we come to it.' My next stop was Mrs Ruprani Parikh.

A Marriage of Beautiful Minds

Mrs Parikh, expectedly, agreed to meet me as and when I'd be ready to drive to her downtown residence, a long trek from my place in the suburb of Juhu, Mumbai. Finally, the day arrived and I reached her house, a bit delayed owing to some confusion about two addresses, with the permanent residence supposedly under renovation. My first impression of this temporary home was that it looked prettier and tidier than even the better homes of uptown Mumbai. Otherwise, I don't have the clearest memories of the what and the how of it all, though I do have a vivid recollection of being seated at her place with mixed feelings of excitement and reluctance. She, on the other hand, exuded confidence and positivity, which worked to allay any fears I must have harboured. If I experienced the occasional discomforting thought of 'What the hell am I doing here?' her demeanour conveyed exactly the opposite, almost like it said, 'I am here to guide you with exactly what you need to be doing.' Getting straight to the point, she explained the entire procedure that entails, firstly, speaking with a doctor from a reliable fertility centre. In this case, I was told about Dr Firuza Parikh from the famous Jaslok Hospital. Even though I had a decent understanding of this myself, I got an in-depth account of the steps required for the IVF and surrogacy procedures. Here, I understood how differently it works for men and women. We talked at length about two things in particular, 'eggs' and 'sperm'. Yes, the science involved was a new subject for me and the entire explanation of age, fertility and gender, enlightening, to say the least.

The crux of it is that, instead of a marriage, there is the involvement of another set of individuals, one, the egg donor, and the other, a surrogate mother, both of whom have legal rights to protect their interests from any form of exploitation. Despite the seriousness of the medical information, my conversation with Ruprani ma'am was like friendly banter, an orientation with a confidante that helped make things seem more plausible and less overwhelming. We left the real intricacies for the doctor to explain further, both as far as the medical and legal aspects were concerned. Speaking of the law, it was heartening to know that this remarkable and apparently not very tedious procedure of making an almost forty-year-old single man, in this case your author, a father, would be absolutely legal.

Mrs Parikh next spoke about her daughter Rutu's experience with the whole single parenting thing and how happy she was to have a grandchild in Ahilya. It was kind of her to also speak freely about what motivated Rutu to take the plunge and how they, together as a family, followed the medical instructions to the T. What I gleaned from these insights was that besides having a thorough understanding of the science behind it all, it was important for me to take timely and sharp decisions at every juncture. Basically, I had to be on the same page as my doctor at every step in order to give this my best shot and make a success of every milestone along the way. The best part of this rendezvous was that one-year-old Ahilya was sleeping in the next room, and I was allowed to have a proper glimpse of this wonder child. A beautiful sight of her resting in her cot probably brought me closest to knowing what I should be doing next. God bless her.

We had other, less intense stuff to talk about too, like their plans for Ahilya. As far as I can remember, Ruprani ma'am herself spoke about the questions that could crop up in a child's mind when born to a single parent. She had answers in her mind, too, ones that were straightforward, honest and made this potentially complicated scenario seem simple and not like some Herculean task. In her words, 'If Ahilya asks us who her father is, we will tell her that there isn't one, but reiterate the fact that she is as special as any other child, from any regular family, would be and, most importantly, born out of love.' That made sense and helped me in reaffirming my decision. The next step would be to schedule an appointment with Dr Firuza Parikh for a day convenient to both Ruprani ma'am and myself. Stronger, clearer and more determined to act, I left that meeting with a sense of vigour and positivity.

The truth is that there are all kinds of families in this world, dealing with and making the most of their own individual dynamics. It's only within an atmosphere of honesty, unconditional love and a sense of really belonging that a child feels a sense of normalcy. I realized how that is the closest a family can come to being normal in the real sense, not through appearances or the external satisfaction of stereotypes and notions. Therefore, I had no reason to believe that my child would feel otherwise. Why couldn't I see this before? Because the truth has its own mystical way of revealing itself. It was okay that I was finding mine at my own pace and was beginning to adapt to my own sense of this new normalcy. One day my child would also adapt to my world, my choices, my life, and we would be one. A father and child, but one family.

Really, I don't have the best recollection of the intervening period before I actually met my doctor-to-be. It probably took me a few weeks to reconfirm my decision with Ruprani ma'am and put our last words from the previous meeting into serious action. I won't blame you for wondering at my indecisiveness after so much guidance, consultation and after having introspected, processed and understood what lay in store for me. If you put yourself in my shoes, though, you might understand I was just being human, and a rational one at that. For such a crucial decision in my life, it wasn't unbecoming of me to ask myself for more time, nor was it a mental disorder to take a step back every now and then. After all, a life was about to change. Yes, change forever. The point is, I made it to Dr Firuza Parikh's house for our first meeting, exactly when it was meant to be.

The three of us started off with a friendly chat about kids, education and, of course, the distance I had to travel that day to get to her place. Yes, even the doctor lives at the other end of Mumbai and I realized that I'd have to be prepared to make several more trips to meet these beautiful people. From our conversation, I gathered that Dr Parikh had grown-up kids of her own and that her son had graduated from my university, the University of Michigan in Ann Arbor, USA. Don't kill me for being unsure, but I think I met him with Doc and we spoke about our favourite hangouts at school too. Something about this made me feel closer to my doctor and added warmth to our very fresh association. Gradually, she introduced me to her field of work and how it assisted people in matters related to fertility, through procedures catered to their individual needs. Obviously, Ruprani ma'am had given her a precis of my journey thus far, but I still took the initiative to be frank about myself and my intentions. She assured me it wouldn't be an unnecessarily stressful procedure, provided I was genuinely ready to go forward with it and stayed positive along the way. I respected the honesty with which she also spoke of parenting as not being a cakewalk and how imperative it was to be geared to take on the responsibility. Here, I was pleasantly surprised to know that a few other popular celebrities, like renowned film director Farah Khan, had also used her services to start their family and had eventually done very well as parents. I remember Doc saying, 'Tusshar, Farah has triplets and today she's a hands-on mother to them. You have to be ready to do full justice to this new role.' I must admit being a bit overwhelmed with this admonition, but since I had taken the time to do my homework, I assured her I was on my mark, all set and ready to go.

What followed was a thorough explanation of all that was required in my case, beginning with the IVF procedure that required an egg donor, whose identity I would like to keep confidential, followed by what she called an implantation for the surrogacy. It would be futile to educate you about the whole biological aspect of it, as that would defeat the purpose of this book, which isn't intended to be a science lecture. Not that I fully absorbed everything right at our first meeting. Instead, I requested Doc to keep me abreast with what I needed to do next and assured her my complete support and cooperation. The doctor told me that, in due course, the first thing required of me would be a sperm sample—my sperm sample. Of course I knew what she meant, but the reality of my decision beginning to manifest itself was both hard-hitting and exciting. Yes, that was how we concluded our first meeting, with probably more than enough discussed for starters. I had a long drive back home, with lots of information to absorb and ponder, and many miles to go in the next few months before I could jump in glee.

As I write about the actual medical journey to becoming a parent, I must admit to going back into my WhatsApp chat messages with Dr Parikh to refresh my memory of our interactions back then. Owing to the speed with which it went by, that phase of those few months preceding the birth of my son is blurry in my mind. I'd like to believe that is because I was destined to have it all and took to everything like a fish takes to water. In reality, though, full credit must be given to the doctor and her team for making the entire rigmarole seem so uncomplicated and seamless. In fact, she had me right at the very start when she mentioned that forty was an appropriate age to get into this radical change of lifestyle and responsibility. For someone who always crucified himself with guilt for delaying his family way, her words served as a much-needed extra boost of confidence. I also remember telling her, 'Doc, I don't mean to sound selfish and narcissistic, but I want to be a father to a healthy child, who looks like me, is Indian at heart and has the right potential. How that happens is in your hands and, for that, I trust you completely.' Her replies were inevitably comforting. 'Don't worry, Tusshar, we always do our best and will leave no stone unturned to give you all that you desire through the assistive reproductive procedures in my clinic.' And work hard they did to fulfil my dreams. It was like almost being hand-held through my journey into fatherhood.

In a nutshell, I was informed about every requirement at the appropriate time. In the event that I harboured any doubts over a deadline or had trouble making a choice, I'd request a personal meeting and she always obliged, even at very short notice. Yes, there were confusing moments, but then there were highlights, too. Like the time when I was informed that the IVF had been successful in the very first attempt. In case you're wondering and need better comprehension, this can be compared to a couple trying to conceive a child and getting lucky with their very first effort. Woohoo!

At no time during the clinical procedures did I ever lose sight of the fact that any public announcement from my side would only come after the child had been born and I had the mental preparation to send the right message across. But some time after the IVF and successful formation of embryos, I felt comfortable sharing my beautiful secret with a close friend, one whom I could rely on to maintain confidentiality. Subsequently, it was at dinner with one of my closest buddies, Sunil Chainani and his wife Gayatri, when I finally spilled the beans. As I expected, they were happy for me and looked forward to seeing me in a new role as a father. I remember clearly that we went on to celebrate the good news with sparkling wine and sandwiches, and a wish to see our kids playing together soon.

The next major step was the implantation into a woman, medically termed a surrogate, who would then carry the child for approximately thirty-six weeks. The time had come and Doc alerted me that she'd be going ahead with this in a matter of days. It sounded like this wasn't something new to her at all—little did she know that her casual announcement had set my heart racing. Contrary to my view that I had got acclimatized to a new life with half the battle won, suddenly everything about this independent decision of mine was seeming even more real, fascinating and unbelievable, all at the same time. But life went on and I decided to enjoy that phase, to make the most of having something to do, something to look forward to and, eventually, someone to love.

The day arrived and the embryo implantation went ahead as planned. The report was expected in a matter of days—twelve, to be precise—and in the meantime, something else happened. I spoke to my parents; actually, I spoke to Mom first. I had to do it at some point. By then, I had reached that point where there was no turning back at all, so I felt like it was high time I drop the bomb. Obviously, her first reaction was that of shock and disbelief. Nevertheless, she also understood and respected the fact that it was my life as an adult and that I had to be the master of my own game. That's the beauty of having a mother. No matter how controlling they seem, they can also see it when you're sure of where you're coming from and then easily let go. But like everyone else before her, she too had her own words of wisdom to share—that she and my father could only be grandparents to my child and could never play the role a parent needs to, especially at their stage of life. According to her, I needed to be ready to shoulder the responsibility myself, not expecting them to take over and do it for me. Of course, I knew what she was saying and would never even think in that direction, which is why it was important for me to have taken that much time in coming to terms with what I really wanted for myself. So that was that, but then I was yet to break the news to my father, and I requested Mom to wait a while before we subjected him to this shock—partly because my father was a typical conservative Indian family man who believed in the status quo. I wasn't sure how he'd react, so I wanted to wait a bit longer to deal with that. With so much else on my plate, I felt like procrastinating on what was probably going to be a long battle to convince him.

But like most Indian mothers who can't keep a family secret from their husbands, Mom was no different. A few days after our conversation, she confessed to having blurted out the truth to him out of sheer anxiety and excitement. 'Tusshar, it was too much for me to keep to myself and not share with someone, so I had to tell your father.' I was a bit numb at first, not knowing what was coming next, but mustered up the courage to sulk about how worrying it would be if she'd start opening up to people, one after another. Her response, like always, was in the negative and she assured me that even Dad would keep mum till we were ready to tell the world. So what did he say, what was his reaction? I hadn't in my wildest dreams expected my father to even remotely be okay, at least initially, with something so contrary to the way he saw the world, relationships and Indian traditions. But the fact is that he was more than okay. In his opinion, if this was what made me feel happy and complete, then so be it. Also that he'd much rather prefer I do what felt right to me than succumb to a marriage that couldn't withstand its own weight and crumbled. We do underestimate our parents at times, don't we? Or maybe, once again, it was just God's hand. Whatever the case maybe, both my parents were on board and it was time to sail ahead.

The countdown to the biggest report card of my life, the results of the implantation, had begun. In the meantime, I also informed the doctor of my progress on the home front and requested an appointment for her to see my mother. Now it wasn't just about me—there were three of us, myself and my parents, emotionally connected to the whole thing. Therefore, it was appropriate for me to involve them in the process too, have their questions answered and anxieties dealt with, if any. Doc was traveling in those days and promised to meet Mom towards the end of that month, October 2015, a few days after the reports were expected to come in. This meant that I had some more time for another round of goosebumps, followed by Mom meeting the doctor after, hopefully, every hurdle in that crucial phase had been crossed.

When I look back today at that month—October 2015, when so much was going on—I seem to have lost complete track of the chronology of incidents. At some point before the crucial pregnancy report was out, I also shared my secret with my close, long-time friend Renu Chainani, besides Mom and Dad. Renu and I were at SodaBottleOpenerWala, a popular eatery in the suburb of Bandra. I recall having spilled the beans in a rather casual, matter-of-fact way while seated at the bar, waiting for our table. The otherwise calm and subtle Renu, despite holding on to her usual demeanour, expressed complete surprise. She had that pleasant yet stunned look on her face and was at a loss for words, besides the admission 'I'm in shock'. Today it makes me chuckle, almost sadistically, at the thought of how I subjected my near and dear ones to this jolt. But it also makes me want to pat myself on the back for being absolutely spot-on with my choice of people to trust with the revelation. By trust I don't mean just confidentiality, but also that trust which has everything to do with genuine happiness and understanding for a friend. In that regard, Renu is a true buddy for, despite her shock, she was joyous and genuinely happy for me.

This evening dinner or tête-à-tête with my lovely gal pals, which also included another friend Sonali, affectionately called Bambi, was significant for one more reason, an equally pathbreaking and empowering personal life change. For years, Renu and Bambi have been following Nichiren Buddhism, a philosophy propagated by a thirteenth-century Buddhist, Nichiren Daishonin. They are also members of the modern-day organization that encourages the practice of this understanding, internationally, in an effort to foster compassion and empower faith. They'd been persistent in trying to get me to study and chant with them, even if it was just for an experiment, to experience the spiritual benefits. A few weeks prior to that evening, I'd attended a discussion meeting at Bambi's place to get a feel for what it all entailed. Honestly, for someone who has mostly been averse to any sort of grouping, especially on the personal front, this Buddhist get-together felt totally out of my comfort zone. Also, the idea of sharing my personal life experiences with strangers felt like a gross invasion of my privacy. Therefore, I resisted the idea of venturing into this arena for the most part . . . until that dinner, when something changed.

Later that evening, I was driving Bambi home and I casually complained to her about the pressure surrounding my acting career as well as certain trust issues in connection with a new friendship. She strongly advocated that I start chanting for just five minutes to begin with and see if I could feel the difference. I don't know why, but the very next day I did just that and soon, believe it or not, was feeling clearer and wiser about dealing with many things, especially the toxicity around me that was holding me back from peace and progress. I have continued to practise and study Nichiren Buddhism ever since that day and make it a point to chant daily, an hour on an average, without fail. Not just that, but I also participate in Buddhist activities of the Bharat Soka Gakkai and strive to propagate this philosophy of compassion by inspiring individuals with my own personal and professional victories in overcoming challenges and roadblocks. Today, when my son is four years old, people ask me if Buddhism was the catalyst that spurred me on to becoming such a unique single dad. The answer to that is anything but simple.

As you know by now, I was already a long way into the process of embracing fatherhood by the time this dinner took place. So, practically speaking, as a father-to-be, I was lucky to have struck a chord with Bambi and made up my mind to start my Buddhism journey. Or was it the new Buddhist practice that strengthened my resolve in pursuing this brave path, like a mission to also inspire others and overcome my obstacles? In my opinion, the truth is what you and I believe it to be. For me, both these pathbreaking life alterations have contributed to each other and made me the person I am today. The rest is irrelevant, for it doesn't really matter if the chicken came first or the egg. Agree?

October 2015, that most eventful month in my life, had an equally gratifying climax. The twenty-second of that month, the date when the results of the pregnancy were slated to be out, had me chasing Dr Parikh throughout the day for answers. Finally, that night, once again on a movie outing with friends, I messaged the doctor to find out what was in store for me. The reports, in the doctor's words, were encouraging; the surrogacy process had officially begun. Nevertheless, the road ahead required a lot of monitoring and there was no room yet for overconfidence. However, I had a great deal to cheer myself for and took pleasure in the fact that more than half the battle was won. Really!

Mom met Doc the following week and that meeting too went off smoothly. Today, what stands out the most for me is my mother's calmness in accompanying me to the doctor's residence on a Sunday afternoon, just before Diwali, the festival of lights. I still remember her noticing the décor of the doctor's apartment, which included various artefacts from different cultures. We jumped into the nitty-gritty of all that had transpired up until that day, as well as the dos and don'ts of what was to follow. Basically, from then on, there were at least two of us in charge. A mother and son, both in control of the goings-on, and looking forward to, blissfully, hopefully and by God's grace, a beautiful grandchild.

The next few months, up until the birth of my son, had a different set of challenges accompanying them, most of which had to do with the preparation for welcoming our newest family member into the household. Not to forget how work, particularly the release of my films *Kyaa Kool Hain Hum 3* and *Mastizaade*, kept me busy after the good news about the successful pregnancy. If anyone reading this is an avid Bollywood film viewer, he/she might recall the unending war between these two films and their producers to be first to the cinemas. I'll leave that war and its aftermath for another day or maybe another book.

However, what matters here is that *Kyaa Kool* . . . made it to the cinemas first, on 26 January 2016, with *Mastizaade* following closely on its heels one week later. Sadly, though, despite their encouraging start, both films saw collections decrease through their opening days once news about the double entendres having been censored spread. Clearly, all the hard work, stress and the long waiting game were to no avail, with the target audience of adult comedies feeling cheated of all that they had expected from the trailers. Despite the huge disappointment, I found the resilience to move on to other, more rewarding aspects of my life, like the baby on its way. Also, a part of me found solace in the fact that the never-ending saga of these two movies was finally behind me, like some sort of karmic retribution with better times to come.

After about two months or so of enjoying professional freedom in Mumbai, I darted back to Michigan for a much-needed break and some important shopping. By important, I mean the necessary clothes shopping that needed to be done for the arrival of my child. Yes, a beautiful memory comes back here of myself in a baby clothing store, which was otherwise full of mothers, looking for sizes that'd do justice to my baby. T-shirts, night suits, gloves, bibs, shoes, you name it, I had them all covered. I would get 'awwws' from peeping moms who'd have their hearts melting seeing a man in his late thirties shop for his blessing from God. With no clue about the sex of the baby, I'd choose colours that'd work for both boys and girls. What fun!

Once back in India, it was time to designate and design a space at home for the baby's nursery. This was when my mom called me up and reprimanded me for not having shared our family secret with my sister Ekta, as we were only a few months away from the child's birth. Agreed, it was high time everyone from the immediate family was aware of the new personal development at home, so I informed my sister that I wanted to see her for a short, important chat, and reached the Balaji office. My sister and I are like friends who can talk about anything under the sun, so it didn't require me to sum up courage or mince words before telling her the truth. 'Ekta, I'm having a child through surrogacy, so I wanted to share the good news with you and also discuss some changes that need to be made at home, especially the living room that we share on our floor being converted into a baby nursery.' Predictably, having expected a professional conversation, she was shocked at first and then expressed pleasant surprise and joy at knowing that she was finally going to become a *bua*, the Indian term used for 'father's sister'. She also understood my reasons for the utmost secrecy with which I revealed my cards, even to family members: to maintain the sanctity of the whole exercise till the time was right for the world to know it all. More than anything else, what excited and amused her the most was the fact that my child would arrive around the end of May or early June, and so would probably be a Gemini like her. With another responsibility ticked off my list, I felt rejuvenated, accomplished and could hear only one song playing in my mind, 'Another One Bites the Dust'.

I did make another trip to the Parikh home to get some final lessons in the dos and don'ts of parenting a newborn. This was that one time, amid an extended period of fun and excitement, when I did get a bit nervous. Most of it had to do with how Rutu kept her home, her baby's nursery and other necessities so organized and sanitized. I felt insecure and realized the need to work much harder on my own efforts. She also had everything from the baby's nutrition, toiletries and routine to the nurse-in-charge, all figured out to perfection. I still remember her showing me how to clean the baby's milk bottle in a manner that left absolutely no room for germs or infection. Above all, she helped me with my research into the right substitute for mother's milk, believed to be the best for babies, since antibodies from the mother pass to the child through breast milk. I was advised to go for specific brands of milk powder that have all the necessary nutrients a baby's milk feed would require.

Somewhere during this guidance tour, I gave up on the idea of trying to emulate Rutu and moved on to other worrying thoughts. At the risk of sounding monotonous, everything about her dedication, somehow, for the umpteenth time, also reminded me of the gravity surrounding the arrival of my own biological child in a matter of weeks. So, instead of brooding over my own doubts, I broke the ice during lunch and asked Rutu whether her life had become more challenging with parenting, especially single parenting. Basically, things like, 'Does one get the time to socialize? Do you get the time to have a life of your own, to date someone, etc.?' I don't remember her exact words but I do recall feeling reassured about having done the right thing besides an understanding of how parenting, even at its most consuming, is rewarding, to say the least, though by no stretch of the imagination is it a cakewalk. Phew!

This lovely family was gracious enough to lend me the cot their little one had just grown out of, besides toys, books and, above all, tons of useful advice. For all those months, during the entire process, they'd become like my extended family. So, with their support, why did I have to worry about not being married? There was a marriage happening, beginning right from the time I visited Tirupati, a marriage of another kind that was making it work for me. A marriage of beautiful minds.

The Arrival of a New Dawn

Time flew by and the living room on my floor within the family home was converted into a baby's nursery. My super mom took charge of everything—from the wallpaper and flooring to the curtains—and she also reorganized the layout of the furniture, with the baby's cot placed correctly, while keeping enough room for a play area. Kudos to her for having done a swell job of the rejig, for the new living space looked and felt like a really cute nursery. This is one area I would've surely fallen behind in. Of course, she had her own experience to fall back on, something we both relied on even while making a final list of all that needed to be procured for the arrival of the little angel. We took a second opinion, too, to make sure no stone had been left unturned, at least with regard to the necessities. With an overload of information from everybody, I remember dismissing some of the items suggested, like a special camera for the baby's cot, which I rejected simply out of exasperation at not having the technological know-how.

On the other hand, some of the items on my to-do list were remarkable modern additions, in stark contrast to the era that I was born in. To begin with, music that enhances the intelligence quotient of a newborn child. Yes, I was advised that listening to Mozart's music was listening to the art of a genius and might therefore give rise to another one. Consequently, a couple of 'baby Mozart' CDs were ordered online. Don't ask me why I stuck to the old ways and didn't download the music—that's just me. We had a simple music system installed in the nursery, with some Indian devotional music CDs suggested by my mother and the new instrumental stuff that arrived a few days later. Perfect, at least for now.

The other fantastic new development of the time came in the form of a baby nurse, a caretaker for a newborn child. In my childhood, most families in India had domestic caregivers for their babies, who'd live with these families and also double as house help. Yes, a glaring example of the social inequalities prevalent in a country like ours. The system still exists, but we have progressed in many ways with childcare. Nowadays, one has the option of employing a trained nurse who can nurture one's child with the utmost care and professionalism during her scheduled working hours, giving parents time for multitasking and working amid a new life. For someone like your author, at the threshold of single parenting, the idea appeared to be a blessing, one that would enable me to have a life of my own and be a hands-on parent, both, at the same time. So, in my quest for suitable nurses for the baby, I began by taking references from young mothers like Rutu Parikh. Here, too, I worked in tandem with Mom to study the options we had and interviewed a few before we zeroed in on two ladies, who'd join as a day and a night nurse, respectively. This whole situation was new and overwhelming, but I guess that's how it worked and was supposed to play out for me, too. The trick is to book the nurse of your choice well in advance of the child's birth, in order to have her start from the time the baby comes home. And so we did just that. From what I learned, the only potential glitch is a situation where the lady changes her mind for some reason, perhaps the distance from her home or even just the vibe she gets. However, we were lucky to have avoided that and were armed with two nurses, waiting for our time.

The icing on the cake was having cameras installed in the nursery to monitor the child from any place that had an internet connection. The only prerequisite is to have the appropriate software downloaded on your device, to make it compatible with the nursery cam, and the rest is pure technological magic. Of course, the idea of being able to see what was going on in the nursery, even when one was away for work or stuck in traffic, sounded wonderful. So we did the needful when we were about a month away from the expected delivery.

They say it feels like time goes by faster as you grow older. I could confidently say that in the year gone by, I had finally grown up, with even more to come. However, after years of struggling like everyone else does on that rocky road called adulthood, I didn't know that growing up would be so exciting. I guess that's what the last one year had been. The final few weeks, before my son came into my arms, were all about just waiting for the big day to arrive. Of course I was still nervous, if not terrified, about this bold step that I had taken. But with the most supportive family and a lot of guidance from my doctors, the final preparation for fatherhood couldn't have felt simpler. All I remember after that is that rainy night on 1 June 2016 when my son was born. Obviously, I couldn't sleep. The uncertainty of what lay ahead had finally hit me its hardest blow. A journey was about to end, another about to begin.

I remember being allowed to take the baby home only after a night's stay at the hospital, for purposes related to monitoring the newborn as a precaution. In the meantime, the doctor sent me pictures of my baby boy, ones in which he looked nothing like me, and had me panicking. My mother calmed me down with the knowledge that all newborn babies look like that, simply because of the way they're positioned in the mother's womb, in this case, the surrogate's. Also, since we belonged to a film family, we were advised against coming personally to bring my son home, in order to maintain the secrecy around such an unconventional pregnancy and childbirth. Therefore, I had someone reach the hospital on my behalf in the wee hours of 2 June to accompany a doctor and the baby back to my home. It was approximately 6 a.m. and the four of us were ready in our pyjamas, waiting for the little angel to arrive. And then, the bell rang.

It wasn't who we expected, but sister Suja, the baby's day nurse, who was going to be the second-in-command with caring for the child. She smiled at the four of us, excitedly, evidently having recognized us for the line of work we are in. Suja was calm, confident and had a flair for knowing what to expect and how she'd go about her job, which said a lot for her experience.

Finally, at around 6.30 a.m., my little prince arrived. I vividly recall Dr Fazal Nabi, from Dr Parikh's team, carrying the baby wrapped in a cloth, and I walking him up to the nursery to welcome the newest member of the family into his home. That was it. My biggest, most life-changing moment had finally arrived. I saw my son for the first time, in flesh and blood, and took him into my arms.

Crazy as it may sound, it was a huge relief to look at my son, only a few hours old, resembling me from my time as a baby and a far cry from the pictures I'd received the night before. In all the excitement, the first thing I did was to put the baby into his cot and let him continue sleeping. I think we all as a family couldn't believe that those moments, after the baby came into our house, were actually happening. Everyone just wanted to stare at him and devour the feeling of finally having a grandchild in our house. Eventually, we all sat down with Dr Nabi, who gave us a lowdown of the basic caretaking measures for the newborn, like the optimum hours of sleep, milk feed, vaccinations and the rest. He was going to be our paediatrician, at least for the time being. Finally, I went to see him off. At the door, I had just one final question for him, which emerged from the multitude of emotions churning in my heart. 'Doc, do I have to stay home all the time now? I'm willing to do anything for my son.' I don't know why I asked him that question, like a lost child myself. I must've felt overwhelmed and gotten cold feet as well, as if my life, with all its sudden fulfilment, was also endangered in a way. Although isn't that normal? I would think so, in contrast to not feeling anything at all besides elation, ecstasy and a sense that everything was going to be hunky-dory. The sweet doctor replied, 'Not at all. You're his parent and the parenting style is your prerogative. Of course, it's natural to want to bond with your son as much as possible and respect his space, too, at the same time. Good luck, you will be fine.'

Following that, we all went back to catch up on some lost sleep and woke up to start a completely new life, one that was never the same again and has kept me on my toes right until this day. At this very moment, as I try to write something down, all the memories come rushing back almost like they're scrambling for attention, so I don't know where to begin. I'm trying hard, but I can also feel the excitement making me lose sight of what happened when. The right approach would be to just try and share as much joy as I got from my experience as a new father.

THE NEWBORN IS HERE; HIS FIRST NIGHT AT THE FAMILY HOME!

Sister Suja instantly became a part of the family—at least, my family. She and I were like a team. We'd complement each other's knowledge and try to find the best solution for every situation. The first thing she taught me was the appropriate way to carry the baby, with one hand behind the head to protect the neck, which isn't sturdy until after a few months, the other hand supporting the baby from behind.

I did manage to get some finesse after a few days, but felt safest when carrying my child while seated. That

77

THE FIRST TIME I TOOK HIM OUT OF HIS COT AND INTO MY ARMS!

moment, on the very first day, with my son in my arms and me giving him his feed, is one which will always stay etched in my mind.

What was even more gratifying was when Suja said something about our bond and the feelings she could see in my son for me, his father. Seeing him in my arms, she exclaimed, 'Sir, *bahut* love, bahut love.' I was touched

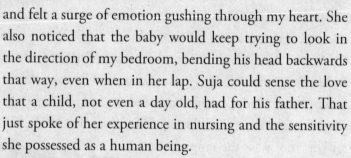

BOTTLE-FEEDING MY BABY ON TIME

and felt a surge of emotion gushing through my heart. She also noticed that the baby would keep trying to look in the direction of my bedroom, bending his head backwards that way, even when in her lap. Suja could sense the love that a child, not even a day old, had for his father. That just spoke of her experience in nursing and the sensitivity she possessed as a human being.

In a few days, I knew I had the right support, at least in the daytime, with me coming in at regular intervals to soak in the joy and be there for my child. Sister also taught me how to feed the baby correctly and at the right times, how to burp him and the right strategies to give him his nineteen to twenty-two hours of sleep in a day. Yes, the first few weeks are about letting the baby sleep as much as possible, with us meant to follow him on his own timetable.

However, the part about actually putting the baby to sleep was almost an art. Sometimes he'd resist for a long time, not wanting to be laid down at all, while at others I'd put him down and then wait calmly for him to close his eyes. As far as enabling him to burp was concerned, I recall Sister and I trying all sorts of things to make it happen, while my family too waited with bated breath. Finally, when we'd hear that 'arghh' sound amid the silence, we'd all go, 'He burped.' Priceless moments we had all been waiting for, the simple pleasures that make life worthwhile. It was all happening better than I had ever imagined. I felt like I was finally living the good life.

The nights, though peaceful initially, turned out to be another story altogether. I won't be diplomatic here by saying that there was another fairy tale happening every night, for that wasn't the case. I'm not intending to sound harsh either, but the fact is that I couldn't fathom what the other lady, our night nurse, had in mind. I respect the fact that, as part of her job description, she had agreed to stay up and work nights as my baby's nurse, but the manner in which it all unfolded in front of my eyes gave me much to be concerned about. I remember her falling asleep for hours on end, something I overlooked on account of the challenging task at hand. Plus the fact that my son was, relatively speaking, an easy child who slept through the night and woke up only to get his feed, didn't require her to stay awake all night, except to be up those few times. Mercifully I was always around too, waking up every now and then to be there for the baby. However, what was alarming and irked me was the callousness that came along with everything else at hand. The way she held the baby tightly in her arms and in a twisted way, with his head falling back, the way she spoke loudly even after he had dropped off to sleep, and the irregularity with which she turned up, drove me to the point where an argument was inevitable. It had to happen, and the night came when she couldn't reason with me. I had to allow her to leave. This happened so suddenly that I had no other choice but to request Suja to return from the train station to double up for that night.

We tried a few nurses after that, each of whom took her turn in doing her best to serve my interests for the night shift, but none of them were like Suja. So in the end, for the sanity and betterment of all and much to our relief, Suja agreed to be a live-in nurse and help me with both days and nights. My son loved her, would cosy up to her warmth and cuddle up to her in her comforting arms. Thus, we found our peace of mind. All's well that ends well.

The days began to fly by as the family got busy with the new addition and our home started throbbing with life. It was a beautiful sight to have each family member play his/her own distinct role in the very early upbringing of my son, with the most passionate, or rather most expressive, of them all being Ekta. She enjoyed capturing these moments on camera—in fact, my entire database of memories comes from the camera that she always had in hand. Sometimes I used to get annoyed, though in retrospect I have much to thank her for. Not to forget the Bollywood song '*Phoolon Ka Taaron Ka, Sab Ka Kehna Hai*', which she'd sing most vociferously to my son, much to my annoyance and in contrast to my subtle, mild-mannered demeanour. Oh yes, it was Bua Ekta who also took it upon herself to find a suitable name for the baby, a task for which we had no other choice in mind. With a passion for numerology, names and the auspiciousness of things, Ekta promised to deliver, and in no time we had a comprehensive list of names to choose from. According to the numerologist she consulted, the name had to begin with L or C. After much back and forth, from hovering around names like Chintan, Lokesh and Lakshman, besides many others, we zeroed in on Laksshya, with a double 's'.

At this point, you're probably wondering how we were keeping the newborn child of a single man at home without an announcement to the world outside. And justifiably so. A secret kept safe within a very tiny group of people was now in danger of being leaked, even before we made any announcement. It was absolutely imperative that the truth be announced to the world in a dignified manner, to avoid the repercussions of any fake news that could be catastrophic to the sanctity of a legal childbirth outside of marriage. I remember my father suggesting the option of having no announcement at all and for people to get to know the reality themselves, to which I retorted that to avoid any speculation and distortion of facts, a formal announcement with unabashed honesty is always the best policy. Even Dr Parikh shared my opinion and said, 'Tusshar, this is going to be about a choice you made for yourself, and therefore, you should own the announcement that goes out into the world; do it without any further delay.'

The fact is, I was always aware of the importance of the job at hand and had been working on a suitable strategy with a friend, a corporate film producer with great marketing acumen. Having confided in her, I also introduced her to my doctor and the three of us chalked out a comprehensive plan. We prepared a statement with quotes from all the parties involved to break the news. We selected a date and a good hour for the big announcement, and she kept an agency at hand to disseminate the news. That eventful day arrived and I reached my office, well in advance of the time chosen. As the moment came closer, I remember my friend taking the lady from the marketing agency in charge into another room to brief her about the facts of the matter and the important statement. Yes, she too wasn't aware of what was in store for her with regard to the announcement. Once I came into the room, I saw the agency girl blushing with excitement, with a smile on her face and a simple line, 'This is big, huge.' The rest of us were anxiously waiting for the clock to announce 10 a.m. to embark on our mission, almost like a spaceship on the verge of its ascent.

The next thing I can recall is the speed with which the news spread, with the ferocity of a lion. Print media, online, television—you name it, we had them all covered. It had to be done keeping the interests of everyone, especially the baby, in mind. Obviously, as I had expected, I was inundated with calls, messages and a plethora of news from the world over for the next couple of days. Family, friends and even relatives who hadn't been in touch for the longest time were frantically trying to reach my family to congratulate us and enquire about the child. I was also flooded with requests for interviews on every major news platform that existed at the time. Honestly, there was ample opportunity to capitalize on the hype to get as much mileage as I desired. However, my intention with the announcement had always been to stick to the purpose at hand, which was only about introducing my son to the world. Therefore, I was responsive but selectively so, keeping my interactions limited to the basic facts. With the job now done, it was time to enjoy the feedback and get back to my new life.

Contrary to all my apprehensions, honestly, there was positivity all around. From the media to the general public and from fans to my colleagues and the film fraternity in general, everyone seemed to be very pleasantly shocked. Believe it or not, it was the same story even on my social-media handles. Barring a minute number of personal jabs and aspersions about me, the rest were just congratulatory messages and wishes for a happy family life. It was heartening to be hailed as an inspiration, with the icing on the cake being the recognition I received as a symbol of sorts of the changing dynamic of the Indian family.

Yes, there's always at least one outlier in every super-successful scenario, which makes one aware of the fact that life is never a fairy tale. I, too, did get my share of toxicity from the most unexpected quarters. A very close family friend's husband, someone I almost grew up with, refused to even send a message, let alone call up and congratulate me. Apparently, he was miffed with my choice of fatherhood and felt that adoption would have been a more noble and appropriate choice. He expressed his disappointment to a common friend, sulking about some belief that if nannies were going to bring up my child, then what was the point of even going this far? The resentment seemed totally uncalled for and more out of some form of envy, so I refused to let myself feel anything beyond pity and total disgust. But I did think about whether being single would make me a lesser father, one who'd rely on nannies to raise my child. Also, if being single and a father was such a crime, how would adoption make the situation sacrosanct? But like the Indian cultural saying goes, *kahin na kahin to nazar lagegi*, so I chose to move beyond the grime and got back to the daily grind, looking forward to the several milestones that awaited me.

To start with, at just about six weeks old, Laksshya looked at me and smiled for the first time. It was an epic milestone of his very early life. Fortunately, I was the one who witnessed it before anyone else in the household and jumped at the opportunity to capture this moment, with a picture clicked on my camera phone. I remember discussing the same with mom, and her sitting beside his cot and stating a fact: 'He is waking up to the world.'

The next thing I saw was everyone trying to humour my son, talk to him and indulge him, only to get him to smile. I shared the news with Ruprani ma'am too. I think it was then that she advised me to go online and subscribe to a site called Babycenter.com, for guidance with milestones as well as with raising a healthy and happy child. One can subscribe for

THE FIRST TIME MY SON SMILED AT THE WORLD!

free by simply filling in the necessary details, like the baby's age, etc., to get weekly updates appropriate to the age of the child, even until the child is more than a few years old. As a matter of fact, I still have their emails coming in every week, and never fail to catch up on anything that is important and practical.

By the time Laksshya was almost two months of age, I had started taking him out of the nursery for a stroll around the house and then to the second-floor veranda of our home. I remember relishing those moments of carrying him on my chest, with his arms and head on my left shoulder. We'd spend hours in the evening walking up and down the veranda, and I would then take him to a hall in another part of the house for a final round before leaving him with Suja to get ready for bed and a good night's sleep. This was the new ritual that filled my days, especially that dreadful time when it's hard to find something to do between 5 p.m. and 8 p.m. Laksshya too seemed to have got accustomed to this new routine that enabled him to get out of his room. So much so that one day, when I couldn't take him for his final round, I remember him crying furiously and resisting his bedtime routine until we took him back to finish the needful. Mom couldn't believe her eyes and exclaimed, 'He's not even three months old and already has a mind of his own!'

The first time Laksshya had a proper shower in the bathroom, the first time he started to eat solid food, the first time he was taken outside the house for a drive . . . I made sure I was an active part of it all. This reminds me of that one question everyone would ask me in those times. It was, 'Do you know how to change the baby's diaper?' I still fail to get why most parents, especially the moms, emphasize this one aspect as being some sort of barometer of hands-on parenting. To me, the more important part was always the time and energy I invested in bonding with my child, as well as the fact that I also made up for any lost time. Yes, I did figure out the art of changing diapers, but the larger picture has always been the reality that, right from Laksshya's birth until today, I've found myself seeking, learning and growing as a parent along with my child. In that regard, I think, I deserve a pat on my back for, in my own way, balancing a structured approach that goes by the book with a more unstructured one that relies on instinct.

Baby Steps into a New Normal

Baby Steps into a New Normal

I'd like to begin this chapter by talking about the arrival of another guest into our house, Lord Ganesh, for the Ganesh festival in September 2016. My family has brought the idol home each year for more than forty years and that year was also going to continue the family tradition, except that it would be little Laksshya's first experience with the festival, popularly known as Ganeshotsav. Eventually, there were many other firsts too, all having to do with my son being the newest member of the household. The living-room area on my floor, now converted into a nursery, had traditionally been the space where the Ganesh idol resided in our house. This time, though, we decided to shift the idol into the lawn outside, obviously to prevent the noise accompanying the puja and festivities from disturbing the child. The plan worked out in more ways than one, with the pandemonium of guests, too, now restricted to the same area outside the main house.

The morning *aarti* for each day of the festivities, which my father previously did, was now mine to preside over. Therefore, with the new baby duties in hand,

I had to manage doing all the religious necessities with clockwork precision, keeping several other chores in mind. On the first day, I remember taking Laksshya for his morning stroll on the same veranda he liked, only to find a flurry of activity, the paparazzi standing on the opposite side of the house, trying to peep into our side. This was a regular feature during the Ganesh festival at our home—they

THE FIRST GANESHOTSAV WITH THE NEWEST MEMBER OF THE FAMILY

were there to capture the festivities this time too, but now found it more interesting to capture Laksshya on camera since until then he'd been a mystery to their prying eyes. Of course, he was a baby and I tried my best to keep him away from those arc lights, but found the next morning's newspapers flooded with blurred pictures of Laksshya and myself. So the first morning of Ganeshotsav was when my son had his first tryst with the glare, however distant, of Bollywood limelight.

That same evening, my mother insisted on taking Laksshya with her to visit veteran filmmaker J. Om Prakash ji (who has since passed) at his Juhu residence. He had been a very senior colleague of my father's, a close family friend and someone whom Mom had huge respect and regard for. The point was for the first grandchild in our family to get the blessings of the over ninety-year-old filmmaker, someone whom she thought of like her own father. I decided to tag along, making it our first real family outing with Laksshya. He took to strangers pretty well and seemed to like the novelty of being outside the house. So I realized I had to move on from the semi-outdoor experience I was giving my tiny tot in the evenings, the stroll up and down the veranda of my family home. It was high time—he was ready to go outside to a park, so I began my hunt for a suitable place to take him every evening for a real outdoor experience.

One of the best choices, or rather a discovery I remember making for my child in his first year, was that of a massive outdoor kids' play area in the vicinity. It started with experimenting on some garden areas nearby and then, almost like God had heard me, I chanced upon my decades-old membership at the famous The Club, a sprawling complex that provides indoor and outdoor recreational activities, including a humongous expanse of land that serves as a play area for children. So after months of enjoying carrying my son, I got him a stroller for the first time and a temporary membership ID card, and we went on to become regulars at this club. That was it, another first. The Club has remained a fixture in our routine, with us visiting at least thrice a week, and continues to give Laksshya the opportunity to exercise his gross motor skills and also socialize.

Everything was going well as a new parent, but that didn't mean that I had it all together and never went wrong. Of course, like everyone does, I made my mistakes too. Like the time when I took Laksshya, barely six months old, on his first international trip to Dubai. My family insisted on us joining them on this trip and I struggled to get the little one's passport made, owing to several roadblocks with the concerned authorities. Now, when I look back, it seems like the more sensible choice would have been to convince my parents of our inability to make it. However, I crunched it all in to make it happen and got on to that exhausting 1 a.m. flight. One can overlook the tiring nature of our flight to Dubai as being a necessary change from the routine life, but what followed was a short three-day trip that yielded little besides the tasks of packing, unpacking and a few moments spent on foreign land. Never mind the mistake; I took it in my stride and now look back on this trip as a miniature joyride. We all live and learn, don't we? So I, too, had to accept the inevitability of ups and downs while making baby steps into my own new normal.

Crazy as it may sound, somewhere around this time, I also started having conversations with friends about possible choices for my son's schooling. I recall taking it very seriously, even when he was four months old, owing to some friends having mentioned getting selected for a school of their choice only because they'd applied for admission even before their child was born. So with some idea about my first choice, I walked to that school and took a tour of the campus to get a feel of the atmosphere and what would be in store for us. I liked the modern vibe and sanitized look of what I saw, but discussed with the faculty that I'd like to enrol Laksshya only after his completing preschool elsewhere. They advised me to start with them from scratch, as they felt that their own preschool students did better in the later years of their school life. I took my time to think over that and eventually decided to go ahead with preschool there, to get my son used to the environment from the beginning. Of course, in trying to be super-efficient, I confirmed to the management of my desire to have Laksshya admitted to their school right away, only to be told that I was approximately a year and a half away from worrying about my son being enrolled in time. Finally, I understood I needed to calm down a bit and decided to wait.

The baby's milestones were happening in time, like rolling on the floor mat and a more structured sleep pattern of taking two naps in the daytime. I was consistent with my own reading habit, too, which gave me insights into modern parenting and watching out for any red flags. Besides online resources like Babycenter.com, I also read a book called *Healthy Sleep Habits, Happy Child* by Marc Weissbluth, MD. Here, I remember that one milestone

I was waiting for in the first year—the moment my little munchkin would sit up and support himself on his own. Having read a lot about baby girls turning on their stomach and sitting up, both within the first six months, it concerned me that my son hadn't crossed that bridge yet, even when he had turned seven months old. I knew the excitement and thrill of having this amazing new job, of finally becoming a father to a gorgeous child, did bring with it a certain degree of paranoia too. Nevertheless, on further enquiry, we were advised not to carry the baby too much but to allow him to be by himself, playing on the floor as much as possible. As a parent who believed in a more normal, natural style of handling and raising a child, almost bordering on the rough-and-tough approach, following this advice was easy, and I just waited patiently for my boy to do it in his own time. Only on the next visit to the paediatrician did I understand that it was not uncommon for baby boys to get up and sit sturdily by themselves only by the eighth or ninth month of their lives. Phew! So nature took its own course and Laksshya, much to our delight, sat up on his own just when the ninth month was ending.

The completion of the first nine months of my son's life brings me to the first film I started working on after I became a father. I'm talking about the fourth film in the *Golmaal* franchise, *Golmaal Again*. After a few months of preparation, mostly the stress of warming up to play the same character in a successful movie franchise after a gap of almost seven years and also pondering on how both work and fatherhood would collide, I began working on the first schedule of *Golmaal Again* in March 2017. Mercifully this schedule was in Mumbai, at the famous Yash Raj Studios, a place not too far from home and where my son could regularly come by. I used my organizational skills to the fullest and planned my own day, within the constraints of my shooting time, in such a way that for a 9 a.m. to 9 p.m. work shift, Laksshya would come over to the studio at around 5 p.m. That is the hour when, under normal circumstances, all shootings halt for a short snack break, and this was when I hoped to be able to make some family time. At times Laksshya had to wait a while for his father to arrive, while at others I was lucky enough to get a break and make it to my make-up room just in time to greet my son. On certain days, it almost felt like my director was aware that Laksshya had arrived and orchestrated a timely break for snacks. I couldn't be more grateful. Father and son would play together for a while and then, when the break ended, I'd see him off to the car and get back to the final hours of work before the day's wrap. I rarely made it home before Laksshya's bedtime, at around 8 p.m., but this short evening rendezvous within the madness of an actor's life couldn't have worked out better.

Looking back, I also remember days when I'd roam around the entire studio complex just to show my son the sights, and that's when he got acquainted with my co-stars of *Golmaal Again*. This memoir would be incomplete without a mention of the interactions he had with my dearest co-star, the lovely Tabu, and our legendary comic star, Johnny Lever sahib. Something about their affection had an instant connect with my son and he reciprocated their love with peek-a-boo, laughter and funny faces. So with all that positivity on set and a work and family life balance, both Laksshya and I were in good hands.

No matter how efficiently I worked out my first shooting schedule after becoming a father, I must confess to feeling a strong sense of relief when the schedule ended. Yes, it was great to be back to work after a while and juggling two enormous tasks at the same time felt like a huge accomplishment. Nevertheless, the freedom to make my own choices after a gruelling filming schedule was a feeling like none other. Here, I must discuss something regarding the idea of parenting and its challenges, for which some clarification is long overdue. Many people have asked me how I single-handedly manage as a parent and have also appreciated my efforts in that regard, especially balancing a family and work routine. My answer to them is that it would be hugely unfair to make it sound like married couples have it any easier than someone like me. At the end of the day, it's all about the choices you make, like the one I made to be there for my son, even after having resumed my work in the film studio. Similarly, I'm sure the challenges and work involved are the same for all parents in any line of work, irrespective of marital status. Of course couples can share the duties of raising a child, but if one area gets worked out, another can get harder, sometimes because of being married. So if you ask me, I respect those married people who, despite the numerous professional and personal chores of their daily life, face the fire and make the time for hands-on parenting.

The flip side to the coin is another viewpoint, which is that a parent like me isn't single if he/she lives with his own parents, the idea being that when the going gets tough, I could always fall back on my own family's support. I do have that option and my parents would love to do more than I've ever asked them to, but as I've mentioned before, life is about choices and the one I've made is to try to be there independently for my child and live my life to the fullest, like any involved parent. So I have my family's support if need be, but don't say I have it easy or have nothing to struggle for, because I do have my own share of worries like any concerned parent would. What I don't have are regrets.

The next big challenge popped up just around the advent of the second schedule of *Golmaal Again* in April. The shoot was going to be outside Mumbai, at the famous Ramoji Rao Studios in Hyderabad, so I had to decide between leaving my son behind with family and taking him along with me for approximately a fortnight. To make matters a bit more complicated, the start of this schedule coincided with my father's seventy-fifth birthday celebrations in Rajasthan, for which my parents wanted to have their grandson join them. Which is also why they were insisting on my leaving the little one behind in their care, for him to accompany them to the destination birthday celebrations and then stay back safely with them in Mumbai. Holy cow! Work, son, family—I couldn't think beyond how to make the three work cohesively and the chaos began getting to me. On the one hand, if I took my son along with me for the shoot, would I be able to give him enough time and, even otherwise, would there be enough for him to enjoy and stay occupied at this distant outdoor location? On the other hand, the bigger question was, what would my ten-month-old do at home without his father for so long? The loving grandparents would try their best to keep him occupied and also indulge him with sweets and gifts, certainly, but that's not what I had envisaged for my son, barring a few occasional times when that kind of pampering is totally allowed. So, it was decided that for the sanity of all, he would accompany his father to the *Golmaal* outdoor set and brave it out with his nanny and father. I requested the film's production team to book two interconnecting rooms for our father-and-son duo, and geared myself up for another rocking schedule of *Golmaal Again*.

The outdoor shoot was conducted in the extremely dry summer heat of Hyderabad, in the month of April, but eventually turned out to be a truly rewarding experience, with hard work and fun in equal measure. To begin with, Laksshya took to the new atmosphere in the Sitara Hotel at the Ramoji Studios complex quite well for a ten-month-old.

OUR FIRST OUTSTATION SHOOTING TRIP, AT THE HOTEL ROOM

The air was cleaner than in the city, the staff in the hotel was friendly and like The Club back home, we had access to a huge lawn by the poolside and even beyond that to enjoy ourselves. Shooting would invariably wrap up by 6 p.m., leaving me with ample time to take my son down to the lawns for a stroll and watch him trying to crawl around his room, before it was time for me to say 'good night' and go. Once again I had to work around my routine to manage my life, like by working out only at night after my son's day was over. As the saying goes, where there's a will, there's a way.

Thankfully, I've saved videos of all the wonderful moments from my first outdoor shoot experience, with Laksshya Kapoor for company and a completely new work-life normal. The play stacks, shapes and sorters I'd carried along, his play mat with alphabets and numbers,

VISITING HIS PAPA ON SET FOR THE FIRST TIME

the lightweight portable stroller: they're all etched in my mind and remind me of all the fun we had, both indoors and outdoors. Here again, I'd be doing injustice to my recollection of the memorable moments without talking about Tabu, Laksshya's new friend on this movie outdoor. It was flabbergasting to see how my little tot remembered her from the Mumbai schedule and smiled at her with excitement and affection every time she came into his room. I also vividly recall her amazed expression at seeing Laksshya recognize her and, in his own way, welcome her, following which she'd always say these three words that still ring in my ears, 'Look at him!'

With all the exposure and fun interactions I saw Laksshya having with even new people, coupled with the fact that he'd begun crawling, I realized it was time to move into another new area: to start play dates with other kids and introduce him to kids' play areas. Consequently, as soon as I was back from my outdoor assignment, I took him to a friend's place for a play date with their daughter. He was a bit hesitant while entering their home, but soon warmed up to the new faces and took to the toy corner in their daughter's room almost immediately. Contrary to what I'd read about kids his age, Laksshya socialized with the mom and a bit with the little lady too, even though she was a few years older, while also playing independently and showing no signs of separation anxiety all along. The only glitch was the part when Laksshya found little or no amusement in the dollhouse and its purpose, sending it crashing to the floor many times and leaving me with little else to say in his defence except, 'Boys will be boys.' All in all it seemed like I was right, so I embarked on a sort of a hunt for all the good kids' play areas close to home.

At that time, at a restaurant, I happened to meet an old college friend who had a daughter very close to Laksshya's age. While in conversation, she suggested I take Laksshya to try out a new-wave kids' play gym that employed a unique concept of amalgamating play with fitness-related activities, to entertain kids as well as hone their gross motor skills. This place, called My Gym, was situated in Bandra, a respectable trek from our place, but she highly recommended it and spoke about kids jumping, climbing ladders and hanging from play equipment, among other things. So I called up the lady at the helm of affairs and booked a time slot for a trial class for Laksshya before registering him for any of the programmes. Soon, we had done the trial session and enrolled into a programme called Tiny Tots which, as the name suggested, was suitable for Laksshya's age. This new discovery was an almost perfect match for what I needed, with my little one bouncing all over the place like a bunny and not stopping for even a moment's breath. The only curveball was Laksshya's restlessness during the starting sing-alongs, when he couldn't hold himself still enough to sit in one place. In addition, the play area was sanitized and spacious, with enough room to crawl and also participate in the various physical tasks that had been set up. So there you go! Once again, there was a will and both father and son found the way.

This was around May 2017, the eleventh month of my son's first year, and I realized how close we were to his first birthday. The whole year had flown by in a jiffy. Of course I was keen to plan a celebration for the apple of my eye, for the day he turned a year old. Ironically, I belong to that breed of people who hate their own birthdays, not because of feeling cursed at being brought into this world, but just for the limelight that comes along with it. The attention is overwhelming and feels deceptive, like it isn't for real, but a mere formality that everyone else indulges in and which has to be borne. My fortieth birthday was a disaster in the real sense only because I couldn't accept my family having a surprise party for me; somewhere I had absolutely no control. Does this aversion to my own birthday and the perceived drama that seems to scare me every year have something to do with the idea of control? Well, I'm not going to psychoanalyze my own mental distortions. I'll put it simply: birthdays don't seem to me as something to celebrate but instead something to endure. Notwithstanding this, somehow I understood the meaning behind the fuss over birthdays only when it came to celebrating my own son's birthday. I guess one gets a much better perspective of things when you're on the other side of the fence. Hopefully I'll mend my ways with time and be more accepting of everything that comes along with the day my parents brought me into this world.

I knew it had to be special for Laksshya and started thinking hard about how to plan it. What was clear to me was that I wanted a very small get-together for this very important day. I had a sense that my little one loved being around people, especially those of his age, but I also understood the reality that small children can get overwhelmed with too many people getting into their space. I'd read about infants having meltdowns, owing to the pandemonium on their own birthdays. So for Laksshya's own happiness, I made it a point to not have more than ten kids on my list of invitees—the very near and dear ones, who, even with their parents and nannies included, would be just the right number to handle.

So, where was I going to arrange a party for approximately ten kids and their caretakers? The venue for such a gathering is of paramount importance, though it didn't take much effort to figure out that the best place for an intimate celebration would have to be the place where we stayed. I had a living-room space at home in mind, but even before we zeroed in on it as being appropriate, I needed to get a party planner for guidance, selection and everything else that a first-time parent needs to do. A friend suggested a creative company that specialized in such events, and I got in touch with them right away for a meeting to discuss the possibilities. Anvi Thaker, an enthusiastic entrepreneur and one of the partners in the company, met me to get an insight into what was on my mind. Having scouted our home for potential party venues, she was in agreement with me on my choice of space as the best option, given the number of guests we expected. Eventually, we selected a list of activities that were popular with young kids and would also not cramp the space.

As we finalized the activities, I felt like an excited father on a little mission to make a success of his baby's big day. Coming to the point, we had a boat theme for the party and the package included the artwork, the cake and a goodies corner with features like sand kits and stationery, among other things. A novice in the modern era of parenting, I was kicked by the idea that an entire makeshift play zone could be installed, and we also fixed up for a tattoo corner as well as a guitarist who'd play songs for the kids. I was still unsure as to whether we needed to add a puppet show to the gamut of items that were already on our plate. Finally, I left it to Mom to discuss those issues that were not my forte, like the budget and the menu. The doting grandmom also decided to add that puppet show for a time slot just after the cake cutting. Phew! I woke up to the reality that planning a birthday party is a lot of work, but hey, I wasn't done yet! Yes, there was still a lot more at stake.

According to me, the most arduous task of the entire rigmarole were the invitations. Since I'd been to very few kids' parties myself, I wasn't aware of the new, efficient ways of inviting guests, one of which involved a three-step process. My planner educated me about the need to send out a 'save the date' card to begin with, followed by the actual invitation with all the details like time, venue, etc., and, finally, a reminder just a day or two before the party. Thankfully, in most cases, your organizer will send you the creative virtually for each step of the process. It seemed easy at first but then, as I started doing my job, life struck and it felt like I had to keep going back to square one. Someone was unreachable, someone unsure, and there are always those one or two important ones who are overlooked by mistake. So the list got a bit longer, though I was persistent in completing the tasks: three huge tasks, if you count the different stages of inviting guests the modern way. Anyway, given your author's tendency to get obsessive-compulsive about being almost perfect in doing things, everything happened in due course and we reached that moment when we were about to celebrate Laksshya Kapoor's first birthday.

I feel excited all over again so I will cut to the chase and talk about the party itself, as I have no recollection of the hours preceding it, besides probably some last-minute chores and the goings-on in my own life. I do remember making a few reminder calls to friends even until a few hours before the main event. Yes, one conversation stands out for me—I was asked by a mother, whom I knew well, if I was aware of the new-age style of organizing activities for a kids' birthday party, unlike the parties of yore when things were simpler and a far cry from the meticulous planning of today. She was concerned about my being a new parent, but I'm inclined to assume that the root cause of the enquiry stemmed from a bias against a single parent, that too an actor and a man. I didn't bother much, though, and thoroughly enjoyed her reaction on being told about all the entertainment planned and about to unfold that evening. So, as I said, there was a certain pride in making this day special for my child, but now I was getting some sadistic pleasure, too, in letting others know that it didn't matter what kind of a family

AWAITING OUR GUESTS FOR HIS FIRST BIRTHDAY PARTY

structure one had—the real fun was in being different and still making it work.

My goosebumps had started by the time it was 4 p.m., and there were more than even the few times I had entertained people for my own events. I was looking forward to this day, so I didn't know why I felt nervous all of a sudden. At times, it was about how many people would really show up from such a small list of invitees to give the party the necessary chutzpah and energy that I so desired for this special day. At other times, it'd be about whether I'd made the right choices for the activities to entertain the kids. And then, I had my shot of espresso and felt ready to welcome our guests at 5 p.m., the first being my own son, the little man of the day, who arrived on time at around 5.15 p.m. Things were calm, with no one showing up for a while, but before I could start overthinking it, suddenly, at 5.30 p.m., almost like a barrage, a lot of moms and their kids came in together, though they'd actually arrived in their own different ways. I heaved a sigh of relief! And not just for the guests having turned up in time, but also because after that moment, I just didn't need to do anything. Yes, for a while I was hyper-aggressive about making sure everyone was taken care of, but with the kids helping themselves to all the different activity zones, it didn't matter how much I said or did, the little bundles of joy were just enjoying themselves on their own. Therefore, all I remember is somewhat of a mash-up of everything happening together, with me trying to be a party to it all. Well, I guess that's what good birthday parties are all about—when the kids feel at home.

Honestly, the build-up to the party is what really matters to me when I write this book—the highs and lows of organizing a celebration for your own son and then watching it come to fruition. Anyway, in retrospect, how would I describe that party? The answer is 'a superhit', for sure! Despite my fears and insecurities, the fact that I managed to give my son and his friends a good experience and came through in my own eyes with flying colours was ample proof that I'd done more than a reasonable job, at least in this first year. Figuratively speaking the party had just begun and many more challenges were still to be overcome, but it felt like I'd smoothly transitioned, taking baby steps into my own sense of the new normal I so desired, and owned it, too.

The Wheels of Our Bus
Start to Go Round

The high of having sailed through 1 June had barely subsided when something annoying and unwarranted reared its ugly head. It had nothing to do with anything that happened on that day or even before it but more to do with the guest list for my son's first birthday party, which had been extremely small. I'd always maintained that only a few kids would be invited for the event and excluded many of my own friends too, most of whom are either unmarried or have much older kids. Therefore, I was a bit taken aback by some friends expressing their anger and disappointment at being excluded from the do. I think a part of the unpleasant twist to this story arose thanks to the presence of the paparazzi outside my house, and the pictures splashed in the media of the guests going in and out of the venue. At the cost of sounding pompous, the fact is that this is a common feature during any celebration at my house, and that day more so as it was my son's first birthday. As a result, some friends mistook the get-together as one that involved much fanfare and a flurry of guests, including many of my friends, if not all. I did try to explain my point of view as being one of a concerned parent who wanted to have something intimate for his son, but the sulking went on and on as if I'd committed a crime. How is it even possible to have your entire universe invited to a gathering of fifteen to twenty people at the most? It was baffling to see that a few found something to grumble and whine about, even those who had much older kids of their own whose full-blown birthday parties I had never been invited to. Ultimately, I chose to focus on the reality that my son would need to have both his own life and identity, and I'd have to try my best not to let them get mixed up with the life I have or have had. As a family, we will have to be together on many occasions, but he would have the right to have his own space too, which was the intention behind having a small birthday bash. The rest is, I guess, best ignored.

So we were now venturing out for more play dates and scouting for newer play areas. The first play date, in the real sense, was the one I organized with old friends Reena Gupta and Kareena Kapoor and their sons, both of whom are around the same age as Laksshya. The moms were the ones who took the initiative and we decided that my place would be the venue. Planning a play date is such a simple task—all I had to do was arrange the toys on the floor and keep a few snacks ready for the kids. The guests arrived in time and we were ready to watch the fun unfold in front of our eyes. Even otherwise, it has always been intriguing for me to watch my son indulge in playful activities, with or without other kids for company. Somehow, I could just stare at him doing his antics and spend the entire duration as if it were a special time. Likewise, on this occasion too, I was keener to do that than chat and catch up with old friends. Additionally, I was also curious to know how my son, not having met the others properly before, interacted with my friends and their kids.

The three boys were fun to watch though, like other toddlers of that age, they played individually and took a liking to different toys. I was a bit concerned as this was also the phase when Laksshya used to be a bit aggressive while playing. Sometimes he threw things and even hit others for fun, a habit that always kept me on the alert, especially when he was around other kids. I don't remember him going overboard that day but yes, there were times when I'd jump in—like every time he pounced on one of the boys to grab a toy or take his place. Between monitoring the three toddlers and their antics, I got a chance to discuss parenting, life, the movies and many other things with my friends. Like most new parents, our conversation too veered towards schooling. We spoke about different schools, from those of the Indian boards of education to the international, the popular as well as the not-so-popular, and tried to narrow down our options to suitable future schools for our sons. Here, I was enlightened about the good, bad as well as the uglier side of Mumbai schooling, all of which came to the forefront of our conversation. From constructive gossip, if I may call it that, I learned about drug abuse among teenagers, to the stories that we'd heard from parents of older kids—the girls and I covered it all. Here, I must admit, my curiosity and early planning for Laksshya and his education seemed minuscule compared to the thorough research that the girls had done. As previously mentioned, I had gotten a bit hyper about this aspect at one point, and had discovered I was way too early in the selection process to get stressed about finalizing anything.

Today, however, the ladies made me feel a bit unsure about my own efforts in that regard, as well as about the scope of my information. This feeling was compounded by one of them also suggesting an early-years programme for tots called Mother Toddler, designed specifically for one-year-olds—even prior to preschool, forget the actual big school! Phew! Notwithstanding my fuss about planning the educational life of my child, this Mother Toddler programme, in my case the Parent Toddler programme, had been completely out of the question for me. I had ideas for Laksshya's preschool years but I'd always disregarded the parent-accompanied programme as being indulgent and frivolous, what one in local Indian terms would call 'timepass', pure baloney. I had heard some mothers talk about it at the park, and it seemed more like a way for them to allocate a certain amount of time for their kids than anything constructive. But that day, my buddies spoke with conviction about what this programme entailed, like singing nursery rhymes, trying musical instruments, art activities to hone the children's fine motor skills and several other cute things. They even suggested enrolling Laksshya into Safari Kid, an international preschool now in the Bandra suburb of Mumbai. I'd like to believe that I have a mind of my own that would never follow herd mentality, at least as far as parenting is concerned, but the conviction of these two women had me totally confused and made me aware that no matter how much clarity I had, I was still human.

The first play date for Laksshya was a short one and the other kids left happy, with the gang of friends promising to meet up soon for an encore, leaving behind a partially disgruntled father who, until then, had thought that he had it all together for sure. Nevertheless, I decided to sleep on the idea and moved on to working on the next schedule of *Golmaal Again* the following month in Mumbai.

Strangely, the whole schooling conundrum refused to let me go and started haunting me in other ways. On one occasion, during lunch with some friends, I was introduced to a young man who had completed his schooling at the American School of Bombay. Though presently living in another country, he was knowledgeable about the educational system here and was aghast at my first choice for Laksshya's big school. I won't name the school for obvious reasons, but I remember him talking about students having it easy at that place. They could do as they wished because of the lax atmosphere of the institution. He meant something about a warped sense of leniency and less diversity, too, that led to the students not developing into strong individuals, prepared to take on the world and chase their dreams with fire and gumption. Honestly, my heart sank a bit on hearing this, but I was seeking more real information and continued prodding the young man for other better options. He mostly just insisted on my considering the American School for Laksshya as he thought it was the best school in the city, but also backed up his argument with the fact that he had his own personal experience to count on, and highlighted the challenges, too, like the distance from my place and the fee structure. He boasted about how this school had a truly multicultural community of students, staff and faculty. Nevertheless, I wasn't going to buy it right away and had something to say to him. I believe that the home is where the educational grounding is established, with most schools being a good resource for further developing the personality of the child. To this, he retorted with the idea that if that was my belief,

I shouldn't be analysing schools at all, that I had the choice to enrol my son into any average government school too. Okay, buddy, point taken.

This lunch, which took place before the start of the marathon *Golmaal Again* schedule, had now turned into a discussion about schools. Despite the intensity of what was said, it was too early to worry—for God's sake, my son hadn't even started walking independently by then. Additionally, the others were in agreement with me that the early years are mostly about socializing with other kids, therefore an unsatisfactory initial choice of school is by no means the end of the world, and can always be changed to a more appropriate one.

I still left that lunch in two minds and decided to do some more research. I called up some friends who had much older kids in the school that I was considering for Laksshya, to enquire about the rumours. The first mom, an affable person and a colleague from Bollywood, was all praise for the school and also spoke about how she'd been suffering these unfounded rumours too. Barring some minor issues, her kids were flourishing there and that's all that mattered to her. She did speak about keeping an open mind, though, as she had plans of transferring her boys into another school, but only if things truly deteriorated. Another friend, a Bollywood wife, related her experience of how this school had assisted her son, who had a learning disability, in overcoming his difficulties and making the cut academically too. She said, 'Tusshar, I had some issues with the teachers there, which is par for the course, otherwise I'm happy with my kids going there as the school is wonderful. In case Laksshya goes there, you will also have your own issues and will deal with them too!' I got my answer, at least for the time being. The fact is, everyone has their own story to tell, so it's important for a new parent like me to follow his own instincts to find the right path for his son.

Between all this and my next shooting schedule, I also got busy doing something unique and literally out of the box. I'd never imagined that besides looking after my child, entertaining and educating him, sorting out his birthday gifts would be the most consuming task of all and that parenting wasn't just a physical and emotional exercise but a managerial one too. With a mountain of gifts, I had to figure out ways in which the little one would make the most of them without boredom or a sense of entitlement. So I devised a plan. One afternoon, when I wasn't busy with other chores, I sat down to open them all in one go, though I wasn't going to let him have them all to himself yet—my plan had more in store. You might think I'm boring, but the best way for me was to let him indulge in a few at one time and then relish the others in instalments, one every month or so. Now this may sound

The first night of
the newborn at
the family home

The first time I took
my son for a drive

His bua's pet

The first Father's
Day celebrations at
my gym in Bandra

Sensing the genius
of Charlie Chaplin
at a park

Attending a
cooking class

Off to Dubai for
spring break

I love you, my
little brother

Attending a
Christmas party

In a tuk-tuk in
Phuket, Thailand

A fun-filled summer holiday

Creativity is the key to homeschooling

Learning the art of fingerspelling

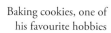

Baking cookies, one of his favourite hobbies

Attending a virtual music class together

Celebrating Ganeshotsav 2020 with family

geeky to you, for I also decided to include a variety of toys each time, like a battery-operated one, a mentally stimulating one like a puzzle or blocks, and a third one more to do with outdoor activities. His barrage of toys and their variety had to be used strategically, at least for an obsessive-compulsive father like me with the best in mind for his son. The unused toys were piled up in another room, where my baby wouldn't find them, waiting for their turn to get on to the floor to be used. The plan was implemented that same day and we were onto something instinctive and super-organized. Hooray!

Between the pandemonium of toys, script reading sessions and other professional tasks, I received a letter from Safari Kid, the international preschool that my friends told me about. Incidentally, they'd opened up a branch a stone's throw from my house and were requesting parents like me to come in and have a dekko. The idea of the Parent Toddler programme had been hovering over my thoughts anyway, so I went online for more information about them. The website had interesting things about their curriculum, which included a play way of educating toddlers by stretching their imagination to the hilt and developing other skills too. My plans for starting playschool for Laksshya only when he was two were now quite shaken up, so I made an appointment with the principal. On the day, I went over to see the place and have a word with the teachers. Even though Laksshya would be eligible for an unaccompanied programme in September of that year, at fifteen months of age, the principal advised me to start the parent-accompanied programme first, for him to get a hang of the atmosphere and because he wasn't walking around independently yet. Following this visit, I also did a trial class with my tot before enrolling us into the programme there. Frankly, I couldn't judge the same for its merits right away, but my instincts were clear that we were on to something good. So Laksshya was now, officially, a pre-preschooler in his fourteenth month.

The next few months or so were like my first real challenge in single parenting. I was shooting for *Golmaal Again* and attending the parent toddler classes thrice a week, at times doing both the same day. On a few occasions, when the timings clashed, I remember sending Laksshya with Sister Suja instead, but most of the time, I was there myself because I didn't want to miss any of

ONE OF THE FIRST FEW DAYS OF THE PARENT-TODDLER PROGRAMME

it. The classes started off decently, with the hour or so moving quite fast amid the singalong and other activities. A teacher sat at one end of the room with us, the parents, and their babies facing her and getting involved in all that she guided and encouraged the little ones to do. Most importantly, the concept served as a very good way for Laksshya to meet other kids. However, the time spent there helped me gain some valuable insights too. I could gauge how much my son had developed his skills by watching his behaviour socially and also got an idea about the things that he liked to see and do in this new zone. I won't deny the fact that I was becoming aware of my own competitiveness as a parent, but in time, also woke up to the reality that every child is different, constantly changing and evolving in their own individual skills. I also learnt the importance of 'letting go' at times when my boy refused to sit and listen to what was being said, to let him do as he pleased, even walk around the room and play with the toys like it was his own self-schooling. I realized that he'd always come back, almost vociferously, to the forefront to resume his participation, as if he'd never left the scene and was listening all along to what was being said.

The first few weeks flew by and this phase with work and school together only got more challenging. Another outdoor schedule of *Golmaal Again* was staring me in the face and I had no choice but to skip school and take Laksshya along for a fortnight at the most. It was okay, really, for it wouldn't have made much of a difference for such a small kid. In fact, a break from the routine can also do a child some good. The principal, though, advised me against making it a habit, as that would defeat the very purpose of a programme that prepared a toddler for the big school. The last time I flew down with my baby, everything on the flight was so smooth that I didn't expect it to be any different this time either. However, a few minutes after the flight was halted due to a delay in take-off, Laksshya had a real meltdown and started to howl as if something wrong was being done to him, so much so that I didn't know what to do. It was concerning, given the fact that something was bothering my one-year-old, who probably got even more exasperated at not being able to express his feelings. I tried everything possible to calm him down, like carrying him and entertaining him with toys. But he just wouldn't stop and the sound kept getting louder and louder, embarrassing me, as my fellow passengers as well as the flight crew were getting disturbed. I was sweating with frustration, so carried him for a walk right to the back end of the aircraft, much to the annoyance of the passengers there. However, nothing helped, not even the small eatables that he usually devoured. So what went wrong? Only God knows. As if He'd seen my plight from above, mercifully, a few minutes after take-off, the little tot calmed down and was back in his usual form.

My co-stars had a good laugh discussing this later, educating me on how Laksshya was probably feeling hot.

They said I should've taken off his shirt to make it easier for him and less claustrophobic in a halted flight before take-off, but what beats me is why they didn't intervene in time, then, to tell me so. This schedule was in the Ramoji Film City outside Hyderabad and with my shoots being irregular, I had much more time than I'd expected for daddy duties. A few months older and wiser than before, Laksshya had the urge to explore everything he saw, so I used the time to take him to all the gardens, parks and shooting set-ups in the Film City complex.

In a week or so, he was daring to leave my hand to walk on his own. Once again, my son and I had interconnected rooms, this time in something called the 'Enter the Dragon' suite. No, we hadn't hijacked a space meant for the Chinese samurai of yore, but Sitara Hotel there has theme-based suites featuring different cultures of the world. With dragons adorning the walls and other Chinese mythological elements forming the interior design, ours looked dark and spooky at first, but with a third living room in between that became our play area, we had much to be thankful for. Talking of dragons, there was also one on Laksshya's play mat and at the time of this

STROLLING THROUGH THE RAMOJI FILM STUDIOS BETWEEN SHOOTS

trip, I recall him having learnt to recognize every animal on it, even the beavers and the meerkats. My reading sessions with my son continued at bedtime and so did our play dates with the warm and lovely Tabu.

THE FLIGHT BACK TO MUMBAI FROM HYDERABAD

Thankfully, the flight back to Mumbai was a piece of cake in comparison to what had happened before, reminding me of the unpredictability in parenting, given the highs and lows that children, like all of us, go through.

Soon, we got back into the rhythm of things. The parent toddler programme had some new facets to its tiny curriculum. They'd introduced various art techniques that required the kids to use their fine motor skills, some so unique that they were beyond my level of comprehension. It was annoying me, the slightly competitive parent that I was, that some kids managed to hold the materials securely within their fingers, to add colour to the drawing, while many others, including Laksshya, struggled to get a grip on their things. Somewhere around this time, I also happened to speak to one of my own schoolteachers from years ago, who mostly asked me about Laksshya and said that I shouldn't start school very early in his life. It was then that I started to question the idea of what I had pursued. I remember mentioning to someone how absurd I thought the tasks were, especially for one-year-olds who couldn't even hold their crayons properly. She replied in support of the programme, saying, '*Achha hai, alag-alag cheezein karke* active *ho jaayega*!' I understood her point as being one of concern: the fact was that the more I encouraged my tot to try and attempt challenging tasks, the more he would learn. Finally, I felt confident about my decision and the whole point of the very early playschool.

Days flew by and the principal photography of *Golmaal Again* also ended, but it didn't get any easier for me, now having to juggle both the promotional activities of the film and school. But I managed it for the sake of my son, even with all the stress and challenges surrounding the release of the big franchise movie. That reminds me of Karishma Kapoor, who once told me what parenting surely does to you—it makes you think selflessly. Blissfully, the film was a huge success, and Laksshya and I both also won the parent-toddler cooking competition at the end of the school term. Woohoo! The icing on the cake was our promotion into the Turbo Toddler programme, starting the following year, in January, when Laksshya would complete just nineteen months of age, as the teachers were of the opinion that he'd progressed enough to attend school independently the following term. Initially, I'd wanted Laksshya to start proper playschool directly in the big school, but the next term at Safari Kid would, I hoped, help him get used to taking on the world without his papa accompanying him. It might seem like I was sorting out my mind and had everything falling in place for me, but that's far from the truth. With all the noise surrounding the pros and cons of different schools and my own second thoughts about immersing my son in a programme even before playschool, I had phases when I was making all sorts of permutations and combinations in my mind about what I was doing and against what I had been hearing and needed to do. Why this school? Why not that preschool? I'd be going on and on, beating myself up, until I'd have to force myself to stop ruminating and go with the flow. Phew!

We partied like beasts over the Christmas holidays and went to every nice children's party in the vicinity. After all, I had a double celebration: my movie's success and my son's first year of experiencing the fun of Christmas parties.

PARTYING DURING THE CHRISTMAS HOLIDAYS

The good times rolled on and we were back to reality in January, with school starting shortly. I was a bit nervous on the eve of the first day, for I couldn't fathom how pressured my son was going to feel the next day, attending two school hours unaccompanied. The first day, thankfully, I was allowed to sit in class with Laksshya for a bit, to wait and watch until he warmed up to the others, before leaving. Initially, it was worrying to have him stuck to me, with several other kids in that class of fourteen having meltdowns that were painful to see and reminded me of my own preschool days. There were also some other kids who managed very well and I hoped that Laksshya would also find his bearings without me. Finally, I left the scene, though once again, was allowed to be in the school area and watch over my son from outside his class, without his knowledge. Honestly, he was brilliant on the first day among thirteen other kids and two teachers whom he'd never met before. Forgive me for being boastful, but I can proudly say that for a nineteen-month-old, he had absolutely no separation anxiety.

Don't kill me now, but I actually sat outside his class for more than a week to see how he was coping. And why not? I'm his father and had a right to do so at that stage of his development, though I never interfered or came to his rescue. In the time I was there, barring a minor hiccup or two, he was absolutely fine. Strangely, he had seemed to lag behind earlier in the parent-accompanied classes with me, but now was managing stupendously on his own. That explains why they say that kids have so many different facets to their personality and develop in their own unique ways. I understood this very clearly at school, with first-hand experience of my own. Soon, I changed my routine from attending the Turbo Toddler class to my morning workout, while Sister Suja waited outside for Laksshya till I got back by 11 a.m., in time to take my son home. The pick-up and drop were a high for me and even a small tête-à-tête with the teachers about Laksshya's contribution to the activities of the day refreshed my mood. Finally, I felt justified about having pursued this very-early-years programme and realizing the importance of trying something first to know its value. I felt more confident about my choice for the road ahead too, but still wanted to do more research.

Interacting with parents, I figured out that it was imperative to tour at least a few big schools before coming to any conclusion. I started that process with a new international school, known for its unique, avant-garde approach to education. The tour spoke volumes about the atmosphere there, in which students were encouraged to think differently, learn differently and even make friends outside their

PEEPING INTO A CLASS DURING HIS FIRST FEW DAYS OF PRE-ELEMENTARY SCHOOL

comfort zone, with little or no room for an academic rat race. Things had really changed a lot since my time, with so many options of a holistic approach to education. Having toured two schools by that time and coming back impressed with both, I was optimistic, though a tad more confused than before. Sad, but true. The turning point in my decision-making process came after a mom helped me see an education counsellor. We met at a coffee shop and spoke with the lady for hours on end. Starting from scratch, she highlighted the importance of first knowing the difference between the different boards of education, like the ICSE, IB and IGCSE, among others, and explained what each one entailed. This helped me conclude that the IB board, with a more diverse curriculum and a focus on personal development that helps foster entrepreneurs, would work best for Laksshya. Thereafter, we spoke about different schools and I was enlightened about how the one I had in mind from before was a good IB school near my place, with the negative rumours being just those—rumours. I shouldn't err in sending my son far away just because another school was acing the current popularity polls, I was told.

I came away from this meeting with more clarity about the right steps for my son and felt like I knew where I was going. The fruitful guidance notwithstanding, I still took a tour of the American School of Bombay, having heard a lot about it. The tour revealed that the students were mostly children of expatriates from all over the world, with only a small number of Indian passport holders, thereby facilitating truly international exposure as part of the education. It also showcased a more liberal, unstructured approach in the teaching style that encouraged research and independent thinking, characteristic of the IB system that was used elsewhere too. The head of admissions and I sat down to talk and I had more questions about the curriculum, but it felt more like I was the one being interviewed, which was reassuring, as the school believes in assessing interested parents on their involvement in the education process. The fact that this lady was from my college home state, Michigan, was besides the point, though it felt like I was talking to someone familiar and that helped somewhat in getting the message across as to why I was there. I'm guessing she understood my focus on a strong foundation for my son through the right exposure and encouragement at school, and wanted me to return to the campus for another round with my spouse—in my case, the grandparents.

She was honest about the lack of diversity there in the socioeconomic status of the students, and also about other prerequisites, like a year of IB education, that make it challenging for students with an Indian passport to be eligible. From my side, I was more than satisfied with what

I saw, the only glitch being that this place was an hour's drive from my place. I left that meeting making up my mind that I'd definitely apply after a few years, at a point when Laksshya became eligible, and then do my best to get him through. I was relieved that the huge burden of making the right decision for my son was off my back. Too cool!

Meanwhile, Safari Kid went off beautifully and we didn't realize how quickly we'd completed the entire Turbo Toddler term, which also included a sports day event and an annual day event, with Laksshya participating in both. School, school, school—that's all I seem to be writing about now. There's more—the summer-school programme that Safari had organized for May—and I enrolled my son in that too. Parenting is no joke, but I was thankful that a year of pre-elementary school had passed in a jiffy and we'd had a lot of fun. The wheels of our bus had turned in the right direction, and how!

When Reality Bites

My son was on the verge of turning two and it felt like he was changing every day. Honestly, following a smooth transition into the pre-elementary school programme, I'd gotten a bit spoilt and had started expecting him to accept and enjoy everything that he was offered. Realistically, what I needed to understand was that my baby was an individual and, most importantly, a child trying to process the world around him and his changing circumstances. Naturally, while developing his personality traits, he was going to react differently from time to time and sometimes even in similar situations, as per his mood and state of mind. We all do that even as grown-ups, don't we? But the slightly paranoid papa that I was, it took me a while to accept the fact that I couldn't control everything. Which is why I consider the next year in my son's life as a year of surprises; some made a lot of sense while others were puzzling and contradictory. But, of course, he always had an over-observant father trying to find some method to all the madness.

Also, I seem to be starting each chapter describing the time around Laksshya's birthday, not because of age but because of the fact that his early school years have always wrapped up at the end of May. Therefore, with his birthday on 1 June, he also begins a new phase in his childhood, a natural pattern that has helped me organize my thoughts while penning these memoirs. After summer school in May, my son and I began the holidays with a week-long music and movement workshop in Bandra. I don't remember the name of the programme, but it had music teachers from a reputable university in the UK that had tied up with a playschool to bring new perspectives and instil a love for art in toddlers. I do remember the sessions had parents and their little ones sitting in a sort of a circle and we'd do various things related to the expression of music, through movement and singing. In the first session, for the first time ever, Laksshya clung to me anxiously and then gradually opened up to the goings-on, especially the new faces he had been bombarded with. There were some interesting moments for sure, but despite a very affable British instructor and her beautiful renditions of nursery rhymes while playing a harp, Laksshya, like many other kids, tried his best to focus every day, but lost interest after a few sessions. We pushed it and managed to almost complete the entire workshop, though I wondered about the point of the whole exercise.

What came as a surprise, a week later, was the sight of my kiddo dancing away to 'Zingaat', the popular Marathi song, with a lot of grace, like he had a flair for music and dance. It was his grandmother who'd discovered his talent, so she'd play the song on TV and replay it over and over again just to watch him. I resented the excessive screen time involved, though watching him dance, I'd learnt some lessons as a parent. Laksshya was going to take to certain events and activities over others, but that was no barometer to decide his innate skills, and so absolutely no reason to give up on the art. When I look back today, I wish I hadn't deterred him from continuing his mad dance in front of the television. A little extra fun and screen time could do no harm; in that sense, I was being the boring one and had been blaming the music camp instead.

The second birthday party was a small, sweet affair, nothing to write home about, with the most eventful part being Laksshya dancing to his favourite rhyme, 'Wheels on the Bus', with his grandfather accompanying him. I couldn't decide who was enjoying it more, the veteran actor granddad or his grandson. In light of all that I had witnessed, who knows? Perhaps the music camp had actually done its job of waking up my son to his inner liking for music and dance, without a hint of it showing up in the actual classes. That was my second lesson: to not judge an activity at face value but to keep an open mind and expose the child to all kinds of stuff for him to try and absorb all that he could. The outcome, probably, is only a matter of time.

I must've gotten really inspired, for believe it or not, on the advice of a friend, I ventured out and got my son enrolled for a week of cooking classes. Laksshya was a bit young for it by a few months to a year, but it was designed to introduce the art of cooking to preschoolers, not some 'master chef' class, so the instructor was keen that he try it out at least once. The recipes were simple and fun to follow, though I found Laksshya not using his fine motor skills enough to complete the tasks. Nevertheless, he seemed to find it all bizarre and interesting at the same time and kept the fire burning, till I'd interfere to speed things up and guide him to the finishing line. The fact that he liked mixing the ingredients and wouldn't leave his bowl, trying to follow the instructions as much as he could, was more than enough for me to continue the sessions, even though he was a bit passive, like a newcomer. The rest of the time, he'd watch me take over and would stay glued to the table till our father-son duo had completed the job. We made some decent cakes and, I think, a pomegranate salad too, but on the fourth or the fifth day, the little one had a burnout and found the open space in the room more interesting to jump around and have fun in. We wrapped up the camp just one session short of completing all the recipes, with the satisfaction that at least we had tried hard.

Today, three years later, my son takes a keen interest in cooking activities, even in online classes, and tries to do most of the tasks himself. He's even chosen to cook something for the Kindergarten 1 assembly video and I'm looking forward to recording that. Once again, like with the music class, it could be that his exploration of culinary tasks many years back had ignited

OUR FIRST TIME AT THE COOKING CLASS

a spark that had lain dormant thus far. It seems far-fetched and funny, but I'm already giving myself a pat on my back.

As I recollect my thoughts, I'm also amused at the chain of events that followed around that time, for we started a messy art class, too, right after we'd washed our hands off the cooking. It might seem like I am some sort of a crazy father who, by now, was trying to make his son do everything, though I can assure you that that was not my intention. I had always wanted to have a regular art session for my son with his friends and a young, peppy instructor from My Gym had offered to conduct a class. The idea was to get a group of kids together and let them have fun getting creative with their fingers and colours. I spoke to one of the mothers who frequented the park and she, along with some others, agreed to come with their tots for a trial class at my house. I'd set up an art table in the lawn for the kids to work on. I didn't even know many of those who had come, but some of their negative attitudes had me wondering about the futility of the effort. The teacher made the kids do what anyone in her place would've done for a messy art class, but soon, the mothers started whispering to each other and gave strange looks, which obviously meant that they weren't too impressed with what they'd encountered. Anyway, that was their prerogative. I was the only one who started organizing the art class regularly for my son and vowed never to indulge strangers. I wasn't being a wet blanket here and have always considered it wiser to let bygones be bygones, but a few significant instances down the years just confirmed my doubts and strengthened my resolve.

We were now in July and had a month to go before big school started, with the Playgroup programme at the Ecole Mondiale World School. After all the hue and cry about which school was good and which wasn't, I'd made up my mind and zeroed in on an established IB school close to home, at least for a couple of years. That way, Laksshya would get acclimatized to the big school atmosphere and gain the eligibility required for me to apply to other schools. Nothing compares to clarity of thought and I'd earned mine after a year of chaos and confusion. But we still had nothing much to do so, with a few more weeks to go, I decided to let my son attend his earlier elementary school in the meantime and then make the jump. He had taken to that place like a fish takes to water for many months, so I was quite sure that this time, too, it would be a cakewalk. Little did I expect that, from loving school on most days, he had now started developing moods and, at times, even resented the idea of being dropped off, till his favourite teacher came to escort him to his classroom. Another reality check for me, I'm guessing, to learn to take life as it comes and enjoy the surprises. But hey, I wasn't complaining either, for despite being sensitive to such changes, I'd started enjoying the challenges of parenting and was ready to take them on.

One would assume that playschool means fun and nothing else, but the Early Years Programme at the Ecole Mondiale World School adheres to the norms of the IB curriculum, wherein even preschoolers of Laksshya's age are groomed for the same. A special orientation for all the parents with the school faculty and an exclusive meeting with the homeroom teachers of Laksshya's class were necessary before the actual school started. The school bag, with essentials like food and water, a uniform for the classroom session and another one for physical education, school-year calendar, shoes, stationery—with everything labelled with Laksshya's name on them— were the prerequisites. I'm sure I'm missing out on some other requirements, but my point is, I almost felt like I was back to my own younger self, just before the new academic year began during my school days. On one occasion, I also remember bumping into another new parent in the school corridor; she spoke of how we playgroup parents would henceforth need to be on the same page and a WhatsApp chat group would have to be created. She was cheerful and excited about it but I must've had a very minor attack of anxiety, anticipating a lot of work for us parents in the days to come, even at this pre-kindergarten stage.

Well, despite the nervousness, I kept calm and stayed positive, and above all, I felt excited for the new phase in Laksshya's life that was about to begin. The day arrived. I can vividly recall dropping off my son for his official first day of playschool at two years of age. By then, I was overconfident about Laksshya's preparedness, having seen his earlier school experience, so I just informed the teacher that I'd stay in the vicinity in case I needed to return for any unforeseen situation. I did warn her that he hadn't started eating independently yet and his having lunch when he was back home in the afternoon was always an option. As expected, the first day was a cakewalk and when I returned to pick him up, he was playing outside with his classmates. In my opinion, he had already acclimatized to his new environment with flying colours and was probably the only child in his class of four who hadn't cried at all on his first day of school.

Gradually, as the days went by, I discovered that there were areas that needed to be worked on. That is normal and probably the case for every child. Here, I must admit with embarrassment that I'd gotten accustomed to the feeling of being a super father to a model son, which was quite unrealistic. The reality that unfolded in the days to come was also an awakening to the well-rounded, holistic approach to education in the IB world—I needed to pull up my socks to complement the schooling with some work at home too. The other two-year-olds were frightfully self-managed and were, as per my knowledge, even off the diaper. Yes, you heard that right. In retrospect, I think I was being a bit too hard on myself in thinking that Laksshya and I were trailing behind in these areas but at that point, I couldn't fathom what was going on with my parenting style. Nevertheless, I gave myself the benefit of the doubt and wondered if it was too early to start such a formal preschool programme; however, better sense prevailed and I just decided to move on and do what felt right and needed to be done. From my experience, if you ignore all the noise surrounding this new mantra of children being self-managed as young as possible, you'll realize it's okay even if they aren't toilet-trained or eating independently at two; they learn these skills in due course.

Otherwise, Laksshya was comfortable, made friends easily and enjoyed most of the day's tasks, so we truly were on the right track, at least for what I'd imagined playschool would be about. Generally speaking, life was rewarding as a father even if I had, for the umpteenth time, turned my daily routine around. With school hours from 9 a.m. to 1 p.m., I'd do my morning workout as well as other work in that time, then rush back from wherever I was to pick up my son.

My days were a far cry from what they were a few years back and another phase in my life had officially begun. Secretly, I must've thanked my son, too, for keeping me occupied, for I was going through a slightly dull phase in my career at that time. I'd done *Golmaal Again* the previous year and had expected the success to propel me to greener pastures, but destiny had other plans to

PLAYSCHOOL BEGINS WITH HIS GRANDDAD PICKING HIM UP FOR THE FIRST DAY

challenge me in that sphere of my life. Besides my son, my Buddhist practice kept me so steady that I didn't even mind the rocky road I was on. It filled me with gratitude in abundance, a feeling of being blessed with fatherhood and the wisdom to see this waiting period in my career as a temporary lull, in which I'd evolve as a human being as well as an actor.

I genuinely miss those days and the simple pleasures that kept me going in a life riddled with imperfections. In a year of many firsts, I'm reminded of the first football programme that I had enrolled my son in, called PIFA Toddlers. It was spearheaded by a female instructor called Anjali, with a towering personality, a way with young football aspirants and, above all, a genuine love for the sport. The venue was a bit of a trek from my residence, but I made sure Laksshya was regular and I, too, never missed a session for the sheer pleasure of watching my son savour the sport in the cutest way possible. Yes, he was moody, a bit lost initially, but he picked up some skills and eventually followed the instructions pretty well. Gosh, so much has happened in all these years and I'm flooded with a barrage of memories, though it all flew by so fast that there are some things that I can only remember in flashes.

There's one person, though, whom I will never forget and would like to bring into the conversation, someone who's been a part of both my childhood years as well as my son's: the one and only Anand sir. A popular swimming coach from the clubs and gymkhanas of my Juhu suburb, I've known him since I was sixteen, during my high-school years, when I'd turned into a hermit who never indulged in any cardiovascular sport, and then gained more than just a few extra pounds of adipose. That's when my mother introduced me to Anand sir—he trained me in fitness and got me out of my slumber, making him my first-ever real fitness instructor. I did learn a lot from him, though after I grew out of that phase I barely saw him until, after all these years, I started running into him again and again. He'd just look at Laksshya and then coax me to have him start swimming, even when he was only a few months old. I did get a bit enthused once and let my son get into the pool with Anand sir when he was just ten months of age. My little one didn't mind this new experience, though regular swimming classes seemed a bit much then, so I waited and did the needful as soon as Laksshya turned two. He had his good and his bad days, but completed most of the sessions to the satisfaction of his coach and also developed an affinity for water activities—even when he'd try to avoid following any instructions, he'd choose to remain in the water and play with his friend.

As far as the next level of group swimming classes was concerned, Laksshya was too young for those, so we stuck to individual sessions with Anand sir to help my toddler gradually lose any fear of the water, with the all-important safety aspect included. Fridays at 4.30 p.m. was our class time, when I'd stand outside the pool to watch my son engage in the beginners' exercises and also play pranks with his coach every now and then. The best part about Anand sir's style of tutoring was his demeanour. He was a friendly coach who encouraged Laksshya's cheeky behaviour as a part of their bonding, while also challenging him with tasks that were daunting and required a lot of discipline. These swimming sessions on a balmy Friday afternoon were my moments of unwinding too for, during that time, I'd have a snack, figure out a Friday night movie to catch up on and just enjoy the calmness around me. Really, I miss those days.

Things only got more intense as the months went by, but before I confuse you, let me clarify that, at this point, there was an art class, a swimming class and the football class in the entire week, all worth every penny and minute of their time. Eventually, I got the right mix only after a friend organized a group of kids to come together for a fitness class, conducted by someone called Hari sir and held in one of the kids' building compounds. At first, I hesitated to take Laksshya all the way there, but as we were already travelling to that side of town for the football class, I figured that this children's boot camp of sorts would be a refreshing change from the regular stuff that we were doing and also a chance to make new friends. Therefore, once the football season was over, we started attending Hari sir's classes twice a week. By 'we' I mean I'd go along too, not because I'm an overbearing dad but, as you can tell by now, it's quite consuming being a hands-on parent.

One has to consider everything—the activities, their pros and cons, the time it takes to get to them—then make it all happen alongside school and without overburdening the child.

Hari sir's classes were very good for Laksshya: he had to play in groups that required him to be social and use those skills to negotiate. Also, he was being trained in cardiovascular activities like running, climbing, hanging, gymnastics and even movements to help improve his flexibility. Laksshya was proving to be a balanced child who enjoyed art as much as swimming and fitness, but had started harassing me on certain days. Dropping him to school in the morning would be an exercise in patience. That was another surprise for, previously, he'd rarely ever shown reluctance to attend school, so I would just start overthinking it, trying to figure out what was going on. Like before, maybe, I was trying to hold on to his past track record with school drop-offs and didn't want to lose my sense of control. But there were a few instances that were truly bad, with my son just refusing to walk through the school complex to his classroom. He'd try everything, from lying down on the floor of his school compound and refusing to budge to even turning around midway and walking out of the school gate. I'd have no option left but to carry him and take him to his classroom. Mercifully, once I'd leave and call back to enquire in an hour or so, inevitably I would be told that he'd calmed down and gotten involved with the day's activities. Of course, I did ask his teachers if something was amiss during school hours and asked my friends too, who are parents, about this unusual behaviour. Everyone just said that he was fine and it was okay for preschoolers to be like that at times. I asked him if something was bothering him about school, but he'd just ignore me or seem nonchalant about it. Finally, following a conversation with a friend who's also a child psychologist, I realized that if there aren't any red flags, it's better to just relax and take each day as it comes—analysing things too much would be a waste of time. By now, I'm sure you must be thinking your author is a crazy man. Well, I have only one thing to say in my defence—to reiterate the fact that I'm a father.

Oh yes, there were also those days when Laksshya preferred to stay back in school and play after school hours rather than go home. On one occasion, I had to wait for half an hour till he stopped resisting and agreed to walk out, but only after his friend too had walked out of the playschool foyer. Then they left together, walking hand in hand. So there you go: children are unpredictable in their behaviour and it's wiser not to judge them for their moods but recognize what's a cause for concern and what needs to be taken with a pinch of salt.

This was also a time when I had some bizarre experiences with a few mothers of other toddlers. I don't want to sound like I'm judging other parents here, as if I'm too cool and have it all together, which is far

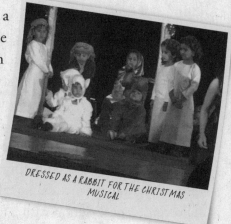

DRESSED AS A RABBIT FOR THE CHRISTMAS MUSICAL

from the truth. However, I can't help but put them in a category of their own because of certain behaviours. 'Tiger moms', 'helicopter moms', 'handbag moms' . . . I've heard all these names before and don't know which would be the most appropriate one, so let's just talk about what I went through and then you can decide what you like. The first experience I remember is of one school mother trying to chat me up each time we saw each other, especially during the pick-ups and drop-offs. I thought she was being friendly and I silently appreciated the gesture, till we starting talking a little more. Gradually, she started asking me about how I made it to school on a regular basis, whether single parenting was tough, had it slowed down my work and so on and so forth. I didn't read too much into these questions and found them just a wee bit nosy, until something happened when we bumped into each other at a club event outside of school. I think it was the annual Christmas party, when lots of parents from school had come with their little ones. We greeted each other as always, spoke a bit about school and then, out of the blue, she asked me how I wasn't shooting that day. I did recognize the cheekiness but replied that it was Sunday and changed the topic, for I didn't think I was answerable to her in any way about my work. But she continued to throw questions at me, one after another, then just stooped to another low by asking me what I was working on next as far as my movie career was concerned. Everything pleasant about our previous interactions just evaporated, and I realized that she was more interested in the celebrity in me rather than the person or the parent. I've kept my distance ever since, even bordering on cold behaviour, because hey, besides being an actor I'm also human.

Another curious cat was less personal about me, but took the cake along with the bakery where Laksshya was concerned. Once again we were at our regular park, this time for a Halloween party, when Laksshya stopped on our way to the main lawns to adjust something with his shoes. Right at that time, a mother walked in with her kiddo and saw us—saw me with my son, to be precise. She blurted out an enthusiastic 'hi', which was very welcome, even though we did not know each other at all. And then the unthinkable happened: while walking, she asked me, pointing at my two-year-old, 'Is he toilet trained?' I didn't get flustered, just a bit taken aback, but smilingly asked her something related to her son instead and then just cut the conversation. What else could have I done? Given her an interview about Laksshya and his progress thus far? You might think that this is a result of being famous and I should accept it all as part of my job. Agreed, but then there's also something called right and wrong. Nevertheless, I hold no grudges and just urge you to accept the fact that my life, as a single celebrity parent, isn't a bed of roses and I have my own everyday battles to conquer.

On the other hand, I've met some lovely people in public areas, too, both in school and outside. There are many parents who, like me, are more involved in their children's lives than in what other parents are doing. I'm fortunate enough to have met such people. So, in a year full of shocks and surprises, highs and lows, I'd found an equilibrium of my own, in a routine made up of my son's school hours, his classes and the evening park time, even though I did have my own professional void to grapple with and overcome. But even here, things took a dramatic turn somewhere in the fourth quarter of the year. The film that I'd been trying to produce for very long and which had undergone a series of challenges and roadblocks for many years—a process that deserves a book of its own—finally saw light at the end of the tunnel. Superstar Akshay

Kumar, who had previously agreed to headline the cast of the film, now wanted to start the film in 2019 and kickstarted the process of setting up the financial structure, as well as finalizing the various agreements. This sudden development was mystical: it must've been the result of some smart strategic moves on my part, or even my prayers and chanting for some divine intervention or karmic retribution. Whatever the reason, I wasn't complaining at all, so, without any further delay, my co-producer and I jumped on to the actor's bandwagon to bring this development to fruition.

So 2018 ended on a promising note, with my film production venture on the verge of a turnaround, while January 2019 continued this trend of sudden developments, almost shaking up everything about my professional life. A web series offer called *Boo: Sabki Phategi*, from the renowned production company Alt Balaji, helmed by my sister Ekta, had undergone several changes in its storyline and screenplay and had been on the back burner for almost a year. Finally, in January, I was told that they were keen to start filming in February and required my dates for that month. After a long wait, I was relieved and excited to work on this horror comedy. I also met an intelligent new director, Dhruv Lather, who narrated the script of an edgy suspense thriller that I thoroughly enjoyed and even said yes to immediately. Clearly, after a brief lull in my career, these projects, some of which were lying dormant, waiting in the wings for their turn to come, chose this time to erupt one by one. Not that it ever mattered to the part of me that loved being a father; I was never frustrated by my professional highs and lows. However, even a doting father with lots of gratitude can do with that much-needed career booster shot to his own morale.

A Roller-coaster Year

January 2019 started with a very lucrative opportunity for my production venture, of a tie-up with a corporate giant that promised more financial security in the release of the film and with a greater share of the pie for the future too. I'm not going to confuse you with the intricacies of how it all works out in the movie business—in fact, we were overwhelmed and stressed ourselves, not knowing how the modalities would eventually unfold for us. Therefore, I had sleepless nights filled with the anxiety of solving the maths behind this new offer, while during the days, I had to multitask with the mental chaos at work and Laksshya's new semester and fresh challenges at school. At one point, I even got the flu because of all the exertion, but soon bounced back to take on the chaos. A period of several twists and turns as a father and the promising end to the previous year now gave way to a turbulent January, one that was disruptive and potentially fruitful too. However, as always, the excitement of my son's life was a stress-buster, and helped me to take on everything that needed to be attacked and conquered.

The highlight of that month was the first sports day at school, at which Laksshya's playgroup class was also supposed to participate. In comparison to the sports days in my time, this one was different, with parents allowed inside the school premises and even seated at close proximity to the main event. You could pep up your child in the beginning, cheer him during the races and even take videos from inside the sports ground. Laksshya had a blast participating—I think he won some races too—but what I do remember with pride is the last parent-child race in which we ran together. Yes, true to my own character and competitive spirit, I made sure that Laksshya and I came first. Finally, to add to the coolness quotient of the times, this programme was a short one and we were home before noon. On the professional front, the movie tie-up became clearer and we understood that we were on to something positive, commercially speaking, so after a few meetings and some back and forth, my co-producer and I agreed to collaborate with the corporate house.

Tough times don't last, tough people do, right? Little did I know that I'd have to hold on to that idea for the rest of the year. So friends, let me warn you about this chapter and what's in store.

January ended with more good news: my sister was also blessed with a baby boy and she named him Ravie, my father Jeetendra's real first name. The child was conceived through IVF and surrogacy, just like my baby, heralding the arrival of a little brother for Laksshya and, hopefully, a future soulmate too.

February was an even busier month, with *Boo: Sabki Phategi*, the horror comedy I'd greenlit the previous year, finally going on the shooting floor. We filmed through twenty-five days of February in one schedule that was fun and energetic, all thanks to Farhad *bhai* (Farhad Samji), the supercool writer and director of our show. Yes, adjusting to being back on shoots after so long and having

LAKSSHYA NOW HAS A PARTNER IN CRIME

my confidence intact took a little warming up, but as you would have known by now, I'm a fighter who'll never give up. Soon, I got into the flow and found my bearings as far as my character and the zone of the show were concerned. This project was all about happy days at work, as the other actors on set were cool too, the content crazy and very much in tandem with the stuff I'd done before. Even Laksshya came on set a few times. One occasion when he had a blast with my co-actors Krishna and Kiku is truly unforgettable for the amount he laughed. They would talk about a fictitious Mickey Mouse in the vicinity, which he found so amusing that it would just crack him up.

I used to be concerned about how he'd react to my sudden absence from home, for I didn't get to see him a lot during the schedule. But I don't recall him missing me too much during *Boo* . . . for, even during the longer working hours, we'd manage to see each other once in the morning and then I'd FaceTime him later in the evening to say good night. The days flew by and before we knew it, Laksshya and I were back together for our evening time at the park, celebrating the end of the schedule. It was a Sunday and I remember that a beer-tasting festival with activities for kids as well was happening in the lawns, almost like it had been timed to welcome us. Such days are rare, when you're exhausted as hell yet glowing in the happiness of professional satisfaction. Above all, I was back with my little partner in our fun and happy hours together. Woot woot!

March started with a bang, and not the good kind. The first catastrophe of the year happened, with the honeymoon phase during the shoot of *Boo: Sabki Phategi* feeling short-lived. My co-producer and I lost out on that lucrative tie-up with the corporate giant, a deal we were working towards for my first film production. The immediate need was to start doing damage control and not let anyone from our side lose interest and, above all, hope. We had to work out another financial model for the film, so I started exploring other options with my lead actor, though there seemed to be no other way but to go back to the original plan before this development took place. Despite this crisis and the confusion about how we'd landed ourselves in a mess after everything was going in the right direction, the superstar was still excited about our film and spoke about his plans for the music, locations and everything else. Phew! Nevertheless, I wasn't going to relax till we actually signed the contracts and started shooting. Until then, another battle, another struggle with this project had begun.

On the positive side, spring break was around the corner and I decided to take my son to Dubai for a vacation, like the tough times had never happened. It was a trip that served as a much-needed distraction for me too. We rocked it at the cool play areas there and came back energized, ready to take on the world. In the chronology of everything that has happened after fatherhood, it seems that my son has always come to my rescue in the darkest of times. It might sound melodramatic, but this also reminds me of what my sister has always reiterated—her belief that Laksshya is a gift to me from God. In Mumbai, we resumed our conversations for resetting the project and after a series of meetings with lawyers from both sides, we'd reached that point of talking dates and shooting schedules. But wait, how could that be possible? There had to be another glitch. Yes, this time the director had some concerns of his own that threatened to become another setback. However, by then my team was well-versed with the art of fighting like gladiators and we ironed out his issues too. Finally, this film had a name of its own and was titled, appropriately, *Laxmii Bomb*.

The first schedule was a breeze and I thought that our struggles with this film were now behind us. Unfortunately, the problems never ended but only got worse, with one crisis after another, to the point that on a few nights I even resorted to mild doses of anti-anxiety pills for some restful sleep. I'm not going to go into the movie's controversies now but, around the same time, I was also thrown off-guard by some issues at the gym where I'd been training for years and hence decided to train in another, better place, though completely different from my comfort zone. My problems might seem to fall in the category of first-world issues to you, but the fact is that I was grappling with multiple issues at the same time and couldn't wait for this phase to end. My reasons for discussing this are not because I want sympathy for what I went through. Nevertheless, I'm proud that even in the most disheartening moments I never gave up and proved to myself that I was made of sterner stuff. I managed to deal with it all and yet continued being a father who had time for his son. Yes, my son's third birthday was around the corner, and I started planning a proper party this time at an appropriate place outside of home. We selected a new play area that hadn't been overused and began our annual ritual of making invitee lists, choosing menus for food and dessert items, planning the return gifts and, above all, finalizing the cost for the venue. With everything else going on in my life this might seem like a burden, but the joy of planning something special for my munchkin was actually a much-needed breather.

The first year of the Early Years Programme play group, for Laksshya, was also in its last month, with a few very cute and interesting events that needed to be attended. I remember the SLC (student-led conference) which happened first, wherein Laksshya had to guide me through his portfolio of class activities, with me encouraging him all along. He mostly stuck to the puzzles he solved in class, though the teachers showed me his entire portfolio of work online. We also did the SPT (student parent teacher) meeting, which we've all endured in our own school years. However, it couldn't have been cuter as a parent doing it for my own two-year-old. The purpose behind these interactions is to get an idea about your child's progress and I think Laksshya was quite a balanced student, even in his first year of elementary school. I wish I could relive those moments with my son all over again—they really were so much fun.

Ironically, exactly on my son's birthday, we also closed every contract that was pending for *Laxmii Bomb* along with all other major concerns, hopefully never to look back at this stressful phase again. The birthday party was a resounding success and for one simple reason: the kids and the birthday boy had a gala time and didn't want to leave. We had to carry them out at 8.30 p.m., long past the time limit set by the venue.

I look back at those months and my efforts with happiness and pride as an example of my own survival instincts. I believe that I could maintain a strong life force, braving many storms with resilience and wisdom, by basing

HIS THIRD BIRTHDAY PARTY

my actions on consistent and abundant *daimoku* (chanting) almost every single day, no matter how busy I was, and regular study as part of my Buddhist practice. Here, I'd like to share a quote from a Buddhist Gosho passage which has always inspired me: 'Suffer what there is to suffer, enjoy what there is to enjoy. Regard both suffering and joy as facts of life and continue chanting *Nam Myoho Renge Kyo* no matter what happens!'

Things got better after that as I started loving my new gym, the workouts improved and I started looking leaner. Simultaneously, the promotion of *Boo: Sabki Phategi* also started on a high note. After an energetic three-week campaign, it was released on 27 June 2019. Like all my movie releases, there was anxiety about the response, especially in the digital world, which takes its time to reveal the true outcome of any show. This was another of the many hectic phases that year when life as a father had me juggling my duties at home and work, both, with an acquired flair that was by now very much a part of me. Of course, there were moments that felt routine, but life was far from peaceful in a year that was turning out to be another roller-coaster ride. Thankfully, my patience and perseverance paid off this time, too, as *Boo* . . . was declared a genuine success after three weeks of its release and broke new ground in viewership for its streaming platform. I was tired and exhausted by then, so I took some time off before my next project, *Maarrich*, a suspense thriller I was acting in and producing.

Every film is challenging for the actors in it, but *Maarrich* was different as it had many firsts for me and that tough reality unfolded only on the job. My director Dhruv is a perfectionist who had a vision for my character, Rajiv, a seasoned cop, and insisted on workshops with the other actors, which is always a good exercise. That's when I realized how much work was needed before I could feel confident about getting into the shoes of Rajiv for the big screen. Alongside, I was also presiding over a lot of things from the standpoint of a producer, like the casting and the music, to name just a few. So the pressure was on and I was back to the grind with another film, another challenging role and lots more to do. This was mid-July and the time to get ready for a new school year was also approaching. School mail regarding the necessary formalities to be completed had started arriving and we were excited about beginning what is called 'nursery' in India.

I think it was just after school had begun when Mumbai saw a deluge of rain, ironically, on the weekend starting on 26 July, a frightening reminder of the devastating floods on that same date in 2005. My son and I were mostly indoors, though I took him to the park one evening when the rains had slowed down for a few hours. I don't know what had happened to me—probably the need for some adventure and some overconfidence, too—for the weather outside was still deplorable. At the park, we sat indoors but then ventured outside to enjoy the breeze and the solitude. I should've noticed that the weather was bad, with intermittent showers that seemed to trick one into believing that they weren't even around, but we stayed outside and Laksshya was even running into the lawns for the experience of a downpour every time the rain gods descended on us. Finally, I had to put my foot down and we left this crazy outing to go back home.

The next night I was woken up by Priya didi, Laksshya's caregiver, because he had been up with high fever and a headache that made him uncomfortable and needed attention. She'd panicked and woken up my family too, who went ahead and called up my paediatrician to make sure that nothing was serious. I was mentally beating myself up for the stupidity at the park the previous day; I administered the recommended doses of medication and tried to sleep but to no avail. Laksshya's temperature was high and given the fact that he rarely had fever, I was stressed. With the added pressure of newer scenes to workshop for *Maarrich* in the following week, I couldn't have asked for a worse end to the weekend. Obviously, we also had to miss school for a couple of days, with the gloomy weather being another downer.

I'm sure it was a way of trying to deal with stress, for I'd inadvertently also begun indulging in more than my usual quota of gym sessions, overexerting myself quite foolishly. All this resulted in a depletion of my energy level. The incidents that occurred in the weeks ahead were quite unfathomable under normal circumstances. While working out on a spinning cycle during the circuit training in the gym, I did not focus on locking the cycle in a break and got my shin scraped by the protruding tongs of one of the pedals. I started bleeding profusely and was rushed to a nearby hospital to arrest the bleeding. Thankfully, with nothing more than a badly injured area of skin, I was still advised regular treatment and abstinence from any excessive movement. So both father and son were grounded at home like sick patients. I continued to attend the workshops for *Maarrich*, though I felt tortured by the inability to fulfil my daddy duties as well as return to my invigorating training sessions. How depressing! Thankfully, Laksshya recovered in a few days' time and was back to school and his friends!

The workshops for *Maarrich* became more intense and with costume trials, auditions for the supporting cast and production meetings all happening simultaneously, the reality of donning both hats as actor and producer for the first time, was beginning to haunt me for the huge responsibility at stake. I'm sure the forces of nature had a vicious plan to test my resilience, for the season of negative events continued with my health deteriorating and a fever making it impossible to function to my full potential. I did bounce back from the fever, though a certain mysterious fatigue had gripped my entire being and, besides eating and sleeping, I couldn't get myself to do anything with gusto. My diagnostic reports were normal and didn't warrant any major concern, but even my doctors were flummoxed by the persistent fatigue and attributed it to some form of a post-viral condition. But did the fever ever indicate a viral infection? I don't know and didn't care either, just felt distressed now about being locked down from doing anything energetic. And no, there was no COVID then.

Mercifully, *Maarrich* was postponed by a week or so, and not just because of my poor health. But Laksshya had to be attended to, so I would push myself out of bed to be with him. I remember waking up one morning feeling well, like I was back to my energetic self, but then had my hopes come crashing down like a pack of cards when I struggled to climb even one floor to reach my son and play with him. I was shell-shocked in that moment, yet I sat down to play blocks with him, pretending to feel fit. He looked at me and then, seeming to have sensed the uneasiness behind my false demeanour, asked me, 'Are you all right?' God! I must've felt my worst then, and was now desperate to get out of this strange tiredness that had gripped me. The clock was ticking and I also needed to get back to work for the sake of my film and my character in it. Alas, I never found a cure for my bizarre situation and till today haven't diagnosed it. I just got back to work somehow, feeling weak, to start *Maarrich* no matter what.

Honestly, I'm as confused today as I was then in trying to figure out the series of ill events that preceded the start of this film. Nevertheless, I was back in my vanity van in mid-August with a few extra pounds and a feeling of being unprepared, yet ready to take on the biggest challenge for me that year: *Maarrich*. I had no choice left but to overlook all the miscalculations, focus on my character and even start training early in the morning to shed the adipose that was bulging out of my cop's uniform. My chanting kept me feeling empowered and, mystically, getting back into the thick of things gave way to an inner resurgence of my health. I guess sometimes all you need is less stress and a little more adrenalin. Of course the story doesn't end there, with several challenges coming up during filming, though I had gratitude in my mind and that was enough for me to face everything, like a mission that needs to be accomplished. My focus was towards making Rajiv come alive on screen, and like this character who comes into his own in the thriller, I too felt like a phoenix coming out of the ashes, both on screen and in my personal life. With my time claimed entirely by the shooting schedule, I had to sacrifice days of quality time with the other passionate love of my life—my little angel. The school pick-ups and drops had become a struggle on most days and sometimes even a FaceTime call to say good night was a privilege.

In comparison to *Maarrich*, the filming of *Boo: Sabki Phategi* earlier that year had seemed like a cakewalk— one quick schedule and we were done with it. Now, the demands of acting in as well as producing a thriller, with a marathon schedule spread over two months, were hard for my son too. We had crazy timings for the days as well as the umpteen night shifts and were battling factors like rain as well as human error in planning and judgement, that consumed me completely. Somewhere along the way, I lost sight of the fact that this might have repercussions on my son and his well-being. He never showed it openly, but his behaviour at school needed observation. His teachers indicated to me that when I made it to school for the morning drop-off, he was fine and stayed upbeat throughout the day while on the other days he was much quieter and even snapped at his friends. The good news was that he continued to score well academically, was toilet trained enough by now to be off the diaper in the daytime, and was also eating by himself. I thought the behavioural issue was just a phase and even tried to explain to him that I was only working and would be back every day, but he continued to be defiant even at home with his grandparents. It was only in the final days of the shooting, when the timings were easier, that I started having Laksshya on set during the lunch break, hoping that it would make life easier for him. And it did. He was more cheerful now, seeing me once in the daytime and then having a regular good-night conversation, too, as part of our new routine.

It's an abnormal life for actors, at least during the filming of a movie, when nothing much can be done with your schedule besides being on set, while our families suffer our absence and wait. But I look at this from another perspective: that Laksshya had now experienced a trying few weeks in his early life, something he could fall back on in his development as a strong and happy child. I believe children also need to face life as it is and understand that nothing is ever constant or perfect. True happiness lies in facing the struggle and waiting patiently for the sunshine that'll come, inevitably, after a rainy day.

Come October, I wrapped up *Maarrich* to be back with my child on our regular schedule, with one new addition to Laksshya's line-up of classes: a LEGO class. Previously, I had been reluctant, for the idea seemed like an excuse to keep kids busy with something that could be worked out in the house. But after visiting the venue of a new concept called COGS LAB, I witnessed the

SO HAPPY TO HAVE YOU BACK, PAPA

innovative techniques that were being employed to fuel a child's creativity, imagination and learning using LEGO. Laksshya *had* to try it out. Soon he had his first class and loved it, and we were on. I also realized he had outgrown the messy art class and could move on to doing something more challenging, like learning how to hold a crayon, a sketch pen or even a pencil, to colour, illustrate and write, respectively. I started the process by teaching him myself how to hold a crayon correctly between the fingers. After a bumpy start, Laksshya started getting the hang of it and there we were, with another milestone almost in our grasp, literally.

I was also fortunate enough to have completed *Maarrich* before Diwali, to be able to attend the annual Diwali celebration in school with all the other parents. Following this, a few weeks later, there was also a parents' assembly wherein the students had to perform for us. At first Laksshya seemed a bit anxious while looking at the parents getting seated in the Early Years foyer, but went on to do his bit with reasonable justice. What caught my eye, though, was him staring at his friends' parents, not really looking for me, but just wondering. I imagined that he'd gotten some sort of stage fright, which I too always had, but it dawned upon me that maybe he was wondering why the other kids had both parents to look out for and he did not.

If that was the case, it was not a problem. It was probably time to start a conversation with the boy about that important 'why'. I took the initiative to address this issue in a calm and casual manner, but Laksshya didn't care much; neither did he respond in the affirmative, almost like the thought had never occurred to him. As a father, I wasn't going to take any chances in case a conflict might have been brewing in his subconscious, so I was relentless in putting the facts out, at least as much as a three-year-old could handle. I explained to him that there would be situations where he might wonder why he didn't have two parents, a mom and a dad, but the fact is that all families are different and have their own unique style in raising a child. So Laksshya needn't bother much, as he had a father who loved him to the moon and back, and nothing could ever change that. He listened to me intently, like he was absorbing my words. Whether or not it reminded him of something about school or I'd hit a raw nerve is pointless, for I'd anyway always wanted him to hear this from his father himself, who was now on the ball and very much in time to address the issue.

After all the madness and chaos, the last two months of 2019 were relatively easier, with Laksshya's classes going on as usual and the season of birthday parties also in full swing. I remember organizing gifts and attending these events with my son all through November and early December. That year, the school had its sports day in December, a

AT A SCHOOL ASSEMBLY
PERFORMANCE

month earlier than usual. I was looking forward to this day and relied on my own stellar performance the year before to pep me up again. However, we erred in not allowing my son to sleep on time the night before and he woke up a bit groggy the next day, not an ideal situation for a sports-day morning. Nevertheless, we reached the venue with a positive outlook, hoping for the best. I must admit, Laksshya put his best foot forward and participated in each race with enthusiasm; however, I'm greedy when it comes to my son and wanted even more from him that day. The teachers seemed proud of Laksshya's sportsman spirit, their main criteria for assessing pre-kindergarten students, though we also noticed him lying down on the open ground, quite sleepy, between races. Alas, even in the parent-child race, we couldn't repeat the previous year's magic and came in second. At the end of it all, despite certain misgivings, I was by now many notches ahead in working out my obsession with perfection, and so was able to see the real essence of what the sports day meant. So I told myself to chin up and prepared to take my baby home, looking forward to another fancy birthday party that same evening.

My family was keen on a year-end Dubai trip, and I thought I deserved one too, so Laksshya and I also joined the others for a week-long break before the Christmas season and rush began. I don't have words to describe how gratifying that short holiday was. I managed to do everything possible—movies, new play areas, dinners with friends from Mumbai, and even slept well, on one occasion from 7 p.m. to 7 a.m.! The highlight of that trip was our outing to a Hollywood theme park that had umpteen entertainment options for kids, the kind that even matched the finesse in my own childhood tours to Disneyworld and Disneyland. I remember getting into the queue for a ride with Laksshya, not knowing exactly what it entailed, and then, after locking ourselves into our seats, discovering that it was a roller-coaster. The shock on Laksshya's face made me fearful for him, though I remember saying a small prayer and just going ahead with positivity. He was quite upset after it was over but we just cheered him for having embarked on a new adventure.

Everything about that vacation sounds blissful, doesn't it? I think the gods must've been merciful to me and wanted to make it a reward for my patience and perseverance after everything that I had faced that year.

ENJOYING DUBAI AND DECEMBER

Lastly, a friend invited me to join her in Phuket, Thailand, for a few days' break, primarily to bring in the New Year together. It's not my nature to be travelling so often and New Year's Eve is just not as exciting as it's hyped and made out to be. Yet, after many years of just languishing in Mumbai with nothing exciting happening, I said yes to her and made last-minute plans to take my son along. I thought it would be a good idea to try out a new place with different options for kids to choose from, like scenic beaches and a boat ride around the hotel lake, things that Laksshya hadn't

IN PHUKET FOR A NEW YEAR'S EVE BREAK

ever experienced. The night flight was exhausting, with a stopover in Hong Kong that lasted a few hours, before we embarked on the last leg of the journey to the island of Phuket. Phuket, in one word, was a revelation.

There was so much more to do than I had expected. Even the hotel we stayed in had activities for kids and organized tickets for us to go to other places, like an elephant park and a water park, both of which were exhilarating, even for a grown-up.

ELEPHANT PARK FUN

New Year's Eve, as expected, was nothing to write

home about; however, I'm still glad I got to be with close friends. I was filled with gratitude for a year that was nothing short of a roller-coaster, with several highs and lows and two fantastic holidays at the end, and hoped for an even more gratifying new year, though a little less tumultuous. When I think about it today . . . if only I knew that the year I was looking forward to was 2020.

The Invisible Enemy and the Lockdown

I don't know how to start writing my memoirs for 2020 for the sheer lack of drama with which it began. I had the feeling of being sorted in my work, with *Laxmii Bomb* in the final round of filming and *Maarrich* having begun post-production with the editing. I don't even remember much about Laksshya's new semester at school after the holidays, besides the regular activities and the pick-ups and drop-offs. However, even in a less stressful time, relatively speaking, life as a father was hectic, with the school hours being devoted to working out in the gym and the career responsibilities, while still being as involved as before in unstructured playtime with my son after school. I had voice modulation sessions every morning, too, to practise exercises for bringing more gravitas to the dialogue delivery and dubbing for Rajiv, my character in *Maarrich*. Basically, a tutor would come and help me out with breathing techniques to bring more bass to my voice while speaking the dialogues. The evenings, of course, were spent mostly in the park or at one of the classes. Some days were quite erratic, owing to my travelling to work events and the wedding of a close friend in Bhopal. Add it all and you've got a forty-three-year-old dad with no complaints, though dizzy and drained from exhaustion . . . and January wasn't even over yet.

How can I forget my nephew Ravie's first birthday party on 27 January, held at a private outdoor lawn? It had a circus theme and we'd organized lots of activities to enthral the approximately fifty kids who were invited. That phase was so full of life for me; I remember styling my hair for the birthday and getting Laksshya dressed to look his best for the evening. However, I also recall witnessing a slight change in Laksshya's behaviour that evening and then in the next few weeks after that. Usually cheerful and happy at parties, this time he seemed reticent, keeping to himself in the first hour. After his best friend entered the party, he warmed up to all the entertainment available. They had a blast playing together, though as a father I could sense that something was amiss and, like always, I was correct in my opinion. He was not himself at school either, moody about mixing with the other students and refraining from many of the activities. As before, I investigated the behavioural issues by questioning my son first. The smart one wasn't too forthcoming with his father, but told his Priya didi, privately, that he was upset with me for carrying my nephew in the birthday party. Okay, so that was the reason for his rebellious behaviour! However, it turned out that

Laksshya had been observing the family's attention to his little brother and the first birthday party plans for some time, and had been a bit resentful of it until the event, with the focus obviously being on Ravie. To his credit, I remember him singing the birthday song for his brother's cake cutting and it was so emotional that I watched the video repeatedly on my phone. He loves his little brother but seeing the family, especially me, expressing the same love for Ravie as for him felt like a betrayal of sorts and the anger had been brewing inside my son for a while.

In my opinion, more than anything else, parenting is about identifying and understanding these moments and then helping the child work out his feelings. Not that I'm an expert in child psychology, but I definitely work at seeing things from Laksshya's point of view and reacting accordingly. I explained to him that my love for him was incomparable to anything else, even after the arrival of a new family member whom I love greatly, like my son. At first, Laksshya seemed reluctant to accept that he was dealing with some intense feelings and thoughts. However, I'm aware that he understands me with depth and intelligence, so I just persisted in doing my job as a father. Soon,

RAVIE'S FIRST BIRTHDAY

he admitted to feeling angry and refused to let me go close to Ravie unless I had his permission to do so. Hmm . . . we were miles away from Laksshya feeling secure in not being the only child of the family, but I knew I was on the ball in at least getting a good start to that goal.

From around Ravie's birthday party, the season of birthday celebrations, film events, weddings and other outings had begun for me. It reminds me of a time when the fruit of my hard work was making me feel content with life and I was happy to go out and socialize. For an ambivert like myself, such times are rare and need to be savoured while they last. Even Laksshya, barring a few minor hiccups, was flourishing in school and his other activities. I facilitated a new art class for him that included pre-writing, tracing and other tasks for fine motor skills, and an energetic new dance class with a hula hoop as one of the props. Those days, he was shying away from joining football in a group class on the lawns. But he finally took the plunge lest he continued to be left out in those evening hours. So now, there were six classes in all: LEGO, Hari sir, art, swimming, dance and football. A few people did suggest that it might be too much for a three-year-old to handle and sometimes even I'd get confused about it all, but with most of the classes in the park and art at 4 p.m. on Thursdays, Laksshya barely missed any of his evening outdoor play in the entire week. So, with a little planning and some luck on our side, the entire rigmarole was now like a cakewalk.

I do remember watching a report on an international news channel about a mysterious viral outbreak beginning from an animal market in Wuhan, China, which had led to the closure of that market and the entire area being cordoned off. It did strike me as eerie and concerning though like many sensational news stories, I thought this one, too, would be sorted out and then just die a natural death. Little did I know that this was a major turning point that would lead to an eventuality that now needs no introduction.

Anyway, coming back to my life, the annual school concert for the nursery class happened in mid-February. Laksshya was excited about performing as an elf, but he had an improving cold to contend with on the day of the event. I could sense that he wasn't his cheerful best on stage, but he was calm, alert and managed to follow the steps, at least most of them, with very little or no stage fright. It must've been an ordeal for sure, but my resilient son went through it all like nothing was bothering him.

Another student's mother, who's a film colleague of mine, very sweetly cheered for Laksshya when his turn came and even took a video of the boys performing. What fun! Weekends were about the beach, a play date and time spent at the grandparents' house. That month,

I was also invited for a TED talk to Laksshya's school and went there unprepared, but spoke with confidence about the topic of dealing with professional disappointments and

PLAYING AN ELF IN THE
SCHOOL CONCERT

came back feeling like a king who'd conquered the world. The good times had really arrived.

My co-producer and I were wrapping up *Laxmii Bomb* with the final shoot of a song sequence on 29 February. I was on the set and had also organized for Laksshya to visit and experience the filming of a Bollywood song, with our hero Akshay Kumar performing a vivacious dance. Now, I must mention here that despite my love for films, I don't watch any at home and neither does Laksshya during the screen time that he's allowed. We listen to a lot of songs but then again, they're not really Bollywood songs. I'm not strict about it or anything, it's just that I'm not as filmi as one would expect a film actor to be, and neither is the atmosphere at home all about my work. However, given my accessibility to so much creativity within the performing arts, it made sense to start exposing Laksshya to things that have been in the family. I thought if done correctly and in the right direction, it might help him develop a passion for music and its expression in movement and singing, that might be useful for his school activities too. Coming back to my point, this is why I wanted him to come over to my set and take a dekko at *Laxmii Bomb*'s climax song, 'BumBumBhole', being shot in the iconic Mehboob studios.

When he first came onto the shooting floor, it was a break and the properties on set were being rearranged to change the set-up for the next shot. Laksshya found the set design that was meant for a beach very entertaining and he started to play with the artificial rocks, trees, lights and sand flooring by running around, picking up things and getting pictures clicked. It was a bit dangerous with wires all over the place and the lights were very hot, so I had to literally chase him down and hold him back. And then there was pandemonium after the break ended, with all the dancers coming in and finally the hero, ready with make-up and in his get-up of a man possessed by a transgender person. *Laxmii Bomb*, a horror comedy, is about a transgender person who avenges her murder by possessing a man who, ironically, doesn't even believe in ghosts. So this song is about the climax of the film, with the hero in the avatar of the transgender person's spirit, dancing in celebration of good over evil and, at the same time, reeling with anger and the thirst for revenge.

I should've realized that to see a man dressed in a sari, with long hair, dancing angrily, might be hard for a three-year-old to digest. Nevertheless, Laksshya was there and it took me a while to catch the strange expression on his face each time he saw Akshay Kumar emoting like he wanted to scare the daylights out of anyone in sight. In one shot, wherein the actor had to swing his long mane to one side to reveal himself and then look into the camera ferociously, I saw Laksshya staring at him, and then after it was done repeatedly to get it right, the little boy must've gotten so spooked that he just turned his face to hide somewhere. That was it for me—I took him out into my vanity van and tried to calm him down by explaining the reality of an actor's job, which is to act. However, he was too stunned to hear anything and just said, 'I want to go home.' I tried distracting him but nothing worked, so I just sent him home to forget about the experience and go to bed. Sadly, even after I reached home later, Laksshya was sitting shocked and expressionless while my father was cajoling him into understanding the situation.

I continued the conversation by explaining to Laksshya that what he saw was part of something like Halloween, a pretense of sorts but in this case, for the making of a scary movie. Gradually, finally, we succeeded in removing the fear of this incident from his mind and all he remembered was the idea that Akshay uncle was being shot in a different, fancy avatar. No matter what, he'd surely had a real Bollywood experience with the drama, dance and music on full display. Not a perfect one, but then that's life. Talking about scary experiences, what followed in March 2020 definitely put it all in perspective.

I'd be fooling myself and you if I said I knew how to begin writing about March 2020 for, honestly, it all happened so fast that I don't know where to begin; therefore it would be best if I cut to the chase and make it as undramatic as possible. One moment, I was out at the Sun-n-Sand Hotel for lunch with my son, followed by a play date, and it felt like the next moment, I was taking videos of him narrating his story for home schooling. The structure of our lives had fallen like a pack of cards as the government started locking down Mumbai city soon after the advent of COVID-19 in India and eventually in my state, Maharashtra. Concurrently, Laksshya's school was also alerting us to possible changes with the rising cases. However, it wasn't long before it had to be closed down and we were down to setting up systems, overnight, for home schooling.

My first day of home schooling was unnerving, the template being one which requires the parent to get the activities done, make videos simultaneously and then send them all to the teachers via email. I remember trying to make Laksshya focus on a story. Uninterested, he switched to another animated video of his choice and spoke about that instead. Gradually, we did manage to complete some of the other tasks that were scheduled, though when asked to go back to the earlier assignment, he looked at me and said, 'I've finished my homework, I've finished my work.' As I got the hang of tutoring at home, the school asked us to upload the tasks on the student's Google Drive, something I struggled with even after stretching my technological skills to the maximum. Finally, after days of continuous emailing, we figured out another solution—uploading the videos on my personal Google Drive and sharing them with the teachers. Confused? I was too, for a while, though I have to admit I've learnt a lot in the aftermath of COVID, becoming technologically savvier as well as more independent. Yet there were miles to go in my metamorphosis before I could rest.

The outdoor recreational areas were the last to close down, which reminds me of my son and I trying to make the most of our last day at The Club. Laksshya's grandfather had also accompanied us, with very few members besides the three of us enjoying those bright outdoor moments of March. There was a certain quietness in the atmosphere, a clear sign of the times to come, but we as a

HOMESCHOOLING FOR MY SON BEGINS

family chose to live in the moment and enjoy whatever we could one last time. I remember posting a picture of my father with my son that day on Instagram, which read, 'The Ides of March are come.' In another week or so, we were fully immersed in home schooling, with me more adept at and actually enjoying the intellectual cat-and-mouse game that I was constantly having with my little brat. Brat, yes, because at times he'd agree to play the chef for a task and at other times I'd use all the tricks up my sleeve to excite him about a story while he'd sit on my shoulders and press my neck instead to try to get me out. Eventually, though, the relentless papa always managed to get the best of his son even though our lives were, naturally, upside down. That's the best part about Laksshya: he has his moods but in the end gets his work done and proves himself a strong and balanced child every time.

Spring break was a huge relief, a much-needed holiday from this new world of home schooling. However, the format of schooling helped me to be more creative with my time-management skills and also find the wisdom to use the resources that were always at my disposal but were lying dormant. I opened

FOR A ROLE-PLAYING GAME

many activity sets that had lain unused for months, mostly gifts like canvas and wooden art, things that a child could paint on, get creative with and reveal their artistic side. The evenings were another revelation: we now discovered that the building compound could be the new park for Laksshya to jump around in, play football and get all his pent-up energy out. I chose to revisit the games we played in the 1980s, in my time, when kids didn't have play areas and clubs to go to in the evenings but had to play within their own premises for lack of choice, not due to a lockdown. So the races were back, the relays were on and hide-and-seek turned out to be my biggest stress buster too. We were also in good company for the outdoor shenanigans—not with Laksshya's friends, who obviously couldn't get out of their homes—but with our own domestic staff, who themselves were in need of an outlet, given the inconvenience and frustration that accompanies a raging pandemic. The World Health Organization had declared the coronavirus to be a global pandemic and the Indian government had announced a national lockdown to break the chain. Nevertheless, I wasn't going to let these circumstances bog my three-year-old down. In our home, with all the things that we were doing, the party was on, at least for my son and I and our gang.

Otherwise the atmosphere had turned quite grim, with an increasing number of infections and deaths all over the world, so I relied on my Buddhist practice and chanted even more consistently to stay calm and positive, and find an inner enlightenment in adverse circumstances. With the strengthening of my faith and in understanding the situation as part of my own human revolution, I turned to social media to help people with ideas for dealing with the stress of staying indoors, besides also communicating many scientific facts about controlling the spread of coronavirus. From posting a video with my son in gratitude for the healthcare workers on the frontline, I naturally progressed to creating digital films of our indoor and outdoor shenanigans, which were both educational and entertaining in nature. No harm in helping bored moms and dads with a few tips from a super-charged father-and-son duo, right? I had so much fun myself, and so did Laksshya and everyone else at home who involved themselves to help us out with the tasks. The bigger picture was finding inner solace, and using creativity and compassion for a good cause.

After the spring break, I found myself struggling with the school's craft activities, especially letter craft, which was regularly on our list of things to be done. Never in my wildest dreams had I imagined I'd be googling methods of doing crafts while educating my pre-kindergarten kid on how to enjoy this subject. To my credit, I always went the whole hog, never giving up, no matter how frustrating it was at times. Letter craft is tedious for it amalgamates two processes—the formation of a letter cut out and that of a picture of a word with same beginning letter sound. Yes, that's how focused I had been, to the point where I started to enjoy doing it myself, almost forgetting that it was something Laksshya needed to get his hands dirty with. Thankfully, I redeemed myself and started dividing the tasks between the two of us, age appropriately.

LETTER CRAFT

We must've covered most of the alphabets in that term and with the other art and craft that was also done, I had to organize our space by discarding the ones that Laksshya didn't want anymore. That was another advantage of the lockdown—it taught us all to keep things less cluttered and save only what was important for the future, while also trying to recycle all the extra unwanted stuff.

The curriculum had us working on the recognition and reading of all the alphabets with loads of exercises that were done repeatedly, like using letter cards to match uppercase and lowercase letters. I don't remember doing any writing activities as homework in that year, though Laksshya was already writing letters on his whiteboard at home and was managing the uppercase letters like a pro.

He had picked it up on his own, probably, thanks to my regular habit of reading books for him. Of course, the grandparents also taught him during his free time. Then there was maths, with the meaning of numbers to be learnt through fun games like 'find the missing number', 'what is more than, less than' and a whole new gamut of funky tasks. We also worked on the understanding of patterns in maths and covered everything from AB, AABB, ABCD to size, sound, colour and action patterns. Trust me, this was very cool and great fun to do. In case you aren't getting a good idea from my description, research it and then just go for it with your child.

MATHS AND PATTERNS

Now, before I start putting those who have an aversion to my talking so much about academics completely off this book, I'll move to the specialist tasks that included physical education, music and dance, a completely new ball game in home schooling and a lot of work.

PE was great fun—simple tasks like doing the different animal walks—and even the warm-up videos that were assigned were great for the evening time and would tire Laksshya out, giving the boy a good night's sleep.

Honestly, he was a little shy about doing the music and dance classes in the beginning, but I'd tell him it was a dance competition or a dance party and then he'd be willing to do it. Gradually, with me and my house help for company, he started to enjoy the

PE

exercise, with some of our dance activities leading to Laksshya's best lockdown videos. I won't be exaggerating when I say that it felt like I was now qualified for an alternative profession, that of a teacher who is adept at doing all the things that the IB curriculum would require.

With all the other pitfalls, the biggest bonus of the lockdown was that I got to spend so much quality time with my son, something I'll cherish for life.

My favourite part of home schooling were the science experiments, wonderfully organized to help a child understand the purpose, process and scientific meaning in the final observation. I must've curated and

ART

posted videos of all the experiments, such as the ice cube painting, the water-and-oil experiment and the making of the xylophone. I did get carried away with some of the stuff and presided over the entire rigmarole while Laksshya, who looked forward to these experiments, was only allowed to help, observe and get the education done. Ouch! We had a downer, too, for the 'whale blubber' experiment didn't work. However, like the two of us, my followers on Instagram understood that the magic is also in trying to get it right and not necessarily in a successful outcome. On the other hand, some superhit experiments had mothers complaining to me about my doing it all and not letting Laksshya learn from making his own errors. Maybe they were just envious of us. Anyway, the point was to have fun with his education and for that purpose, my homeschooling chores were, obviously, on the ball.

I went to the extent of saving up certain tasks that were optional for school and using them for the holidays. The rain experiment was one such activity that turned out to be quite a blockbuster for Laksshya's learning and fun, and it was the highest viewed video on my Instagram account!

PAINTING EXPERIMENT WITH ICE CUBES

Okay, I can now hear you calling me a hands-on father who's also a mad teacher and, above all, a selfish show-off. I'm not denying that I also was swayed and tried to gain some validation for myself online, but the broader picture is that all of us, at this time, were trying to find joy in everything that we were doing for our families and I was no exception.

A ROLE-PLAYING GAME WITH THE VET

Everything was done at home and then uploaded onto a Google Drive for school. We also had the privilege of watching the annual concert at home, for the school sent us the link to the video recording as a part of the weekend homework. This turned out to be a good opportunity for us to watch it together like a movie, with popcorn and other snacks to go with the mood. Laksshya's grandparents never showed him, but they weren't particularly impressed with what they saw, probably expecting some acrobatics from him or God knows what. My darling nephew Ravie, though, was delighted to see his older brother on screen and stood up to cheer him like a total cutie. Laksshya wasn't in the least bit concerned about anybody's thoughts and reactions—he was too engrossed in the video, watching himself with his friends, and even that wasn't enough for he insisted on repeating the same video again and again. Finally, towards the end of the term, the parents got to see the entire portfolio of the year's work at home. Full marks to the teachers for being the heroes of homeschooling and rising to the occasion in circumstances that have had absolutely no precedent. It is owing to Laksshya's teachers that a smooth transition into homeschooling was possible; the rest of the nursery year was completed without any major glitches or inconvenience.

With so much going on with school, the other classes that we were enrolled into took a backseat during the first major lockdown. I think it was just too much for Laksshya to do the dance sessions or even LEGO in an online class and I just let him be when he resisted it all. Children do need their personal space, and Laksshya definitely needed it in those early months of the stringent curbs, when we were already confined and restricted from having a normal lifestyle. I think we were managing pretty well in the new normal, but it was also good to have a schoolfriend who lived in the neighbourhood come over once a week to play with Laksshya, like a silver lining to the dark cloud of a child missing out on socializing in a pandemic like that. Alas, Laksshya's fourth birthday party was also a locked-down affair, with only one friend and the friend's mother in attendance. He didn't seem perturbed at all by the way it was planned; in fact, he was very happy to have just his good friend and immediate family with him. What mattered the most was his choice of the Baby Shark theme and for that, I managed to procure some appropriate décor, accessories and, of course, a cake.

The only thing that needed some work was that my boy still felt resentful about his little brother and I had to keep reminding Laksshya that we all still loved him as much as before, with no compromise whatsoever in the importance that he had in our hearts. There

A LOCKDOWN BIRTHDAY PARTY

were good days and bad days and I think he struggled with his feelings the most when we were together. On his birthday, I saw him looking like something was wrong and then figured out that it was after Ravie, my nephew, walked into the room. Thereafter, unless I distracted him with something, it was hard for us to even get him to smile for a photograph. I was worried that Laksshya wasn't having the happiest time that day, but I believe even these conflicts and their resolutions are a part of growing up. We as parents can only help the child in understanding the true picture. So I cheered him up one more time and moved him on to celebrating all that we had accomplished in the last few months in lockdown. Like always, my mantra was that this too would pass.

1 June 2021 is my son's fifth birthday. I have gone back more than a year in my life to write this chapter about all the things we managed to do in 2020, and I'm feeling exhausted. I was homeschooling, working out in the gym, working from home and then also uploading my son's work for his teachers. With so much going on and not a moment to just relax, I used to wonder how so many people were getting bored and searching online for things to be busy with. Life to me is all about what you make it to be and I'm blessed to have been able to prove it even in 2020, the year of being homebound.

And Miles to Go Before We Really Unlock

The first week of June continues to have the significance of being the start of my Laksshya's summer vacations, like a birthday gift to him on 1 June. What made June 2020 even more eventful was the extensive, graded strategy for unlocking the nation implemented by the government. The timing was right, coming after a gruelling few months of homeschooling. However, not much in our lives changed, except a few things like the beach being opened for a few hours in the morning, which was more than enough for starters, given that we had had our lessons in valuing and having gratitude for even the little pleasures of the unrestricted life.

Laksshya seemed to have matured a lot very quickly. He now found a lot more gratification in helping us with the morning household chores and not just in his playtime, from assisting with the renovation work in our home, especially the parts that required him to count numbers and make patterns for things, to using his creative skills to make a salad or bake cookies for his grandparents. But soon he'd be back to his antics, like applying shaving foam on his cheeks in trying to behave like an adult. He made several trips to the only supermarket that was open in our area, thanks to his grandfather, who indulged his desire for the outing; it gave him a productive feeling of having picked up stuff for the household's needs all by himself. Likewise, this idea of seeking joy and satisfaction from being productive in confinement worked well with adults like myself too. We compartmentalized our day with a structured routine, focused on what made us happy, and tried to create within the confines of our homes all that we could not do, giving us hope and a sense of purpose. Which reminds me of something that a mother had asked me recently. She quipped, 'Has worked started?' I replied, 'When did it ever stop?'

The summer monsoon was also expected. Cyclone Nisarga, the strongest tropical cyclone to have struck Maharashtra in more than a century, came along with it. Besides praying for the least amount of damage in its aftermath, we were also in time to record a video of the rain experiment, wherein shaving foam is sprayed lightly to cover the surface of water in a glass following which droplets of food colour on the foam pass through it and can be seen falling in the water like rain. This was meant to help Laksshya and the other kids understand rain formation, while making a direct connection to what was actually happening outside our windows. In the wake of the storm, I took my son to witness what nature's fury really was like, to experience the sight of fallen trees lying across the road outside my house while also getting a lesson in social responsibility and the importance of protecting our environment. Obviously, he was clueless about the irony of it all happening in the week of millions celebrating World Environment Day but it must've made an impact, for the first thing he said on seeing the carnage was 'Trees *bhi* broken *ho gaya* Papa, trees bhi broken ho gaya.'

The permissible morning hours for free play at Juhu beach were a huge relief for Laksshya in the unlocking process. I never accompanied him and tried to catch up on my own me-time instead, but his caregiver, Priya didi, discovered a time and a spot at the beach that was quiet and they'd have a blast, always extending their deadline after somehow convincing the cops patrolling the entire area. It makes me wonder if our kids will remember the exercise in resilience that they've had to endure since the lockdown started and what it must've felt like being back to indulging in their favourite pastimes. Surely, our state of mind while coping with these challenges must be rubbing off on them for, like me, Laksshya seemed happy with whatever he got and even found room to extend his limits to do whatever he wanted. Like in the inflated pool I set up for him on the terrace of our house, an old birthday gift waiting for the right time to be opened—what better time than a summer in lockdown? With a slide, two pools, a shower system and my darling nephew Ravie joining him in the water, the pool party was definitely back and how! My bundle of joy would also test my limits every now and then, especially when he got into the mood to splash water on anyone who came within reach, even his grandfather, who sat innocently to enjoy the sight of his grandchildren making the most of life.

Speaking of mental resilience, my Bollywood work life continued to challenge me like before, especially with the unpredictability and uncertainty of what lay ahead for movies and their return to the cinemas. After great deliberation, *Laxmii Bomb* was finalized to be a direct-to-OTT release, a huge mental adjustment for your author, who now couldn't tell if his world was falling apart or getting resurrected, in the avalanche of crises that no living person was escaping. Eventually, of course, wisdom prevailed and I understood the advantage of a worldwide digital premiere on the number-one platform in India over a never-ending wait for cinemas and their return to normalcy. Anyway, to kickstart the campaign, I needed to shoot myself holding a ticket for the first day, first show of the film on its streaming platform. I used this opportunity to shoot some pictures with my son, too, making it our first time together for a professionally shot photo session at home.

That day, I saw a new side to Laksshya's personality. For someone who took time to warm up at parties, he opened up quite easily and was having fun trying out different expressions in front of the camera, which kept the atmosphere lively and the photographer in total amazement. He understood the mood for the pictures that we shot together, though it seemed like he was really flirting with the lens after I left the scene and was shooting pictures alone. So did I get a sense of the budding actor somewhere inside my son? After all, that would be a natural reaction to a third-generation filmwala in a family of actors and producers. Well, only time will tell if he's passionate about acting and the world of entertainment, but the circumstances had surely helped us get out of our comfort zone and discover newer facets to my boy and his interests.

Schools were reopened in July and Laksshya was now in K1, with a new phase in distance learning wherein classes were conducted virtually. The asynchronous tasks that needed to be recorded by parents initially were now being done with Seesaw, an app designed for this purpose. With parental guidance for simply encouraging the child during the day's activities, the pressure was off my back, but another challenge was lurking and had me racking my brain. I had to rework my routine to be with my son for the morning classes till noon, so my days began in the afternoon and have remained that way until now, as I write this page a week after K1 has ended. I have observed that my son has always improved his skills and grown more independent during his school breaks and this time, too, the unstructured practice of his academic interests was yielding benefits. He was reading more confidently, had started to write by himself and even enjoyed his baby scissors to cut straight and zigzag lines on paper. I won't take credit for all the progress though I have worked hard on him, but the fact that he was also doing his own work, like wearing his shoes independently, is owing to my timely intervention and insistence on protocols for self-management.

Yes, there were many good days and a few not-so-good ones too—exactly what happens when you have a moody child who focuses on the class activities only when he wants to while at other times he will look the other way even though he knows how to answer an important question. Naturally, I'd be frustrated with this behaviour and even shouted at him on a few occasions, just to get him back in line with his schoolmates. The smart, perceptive boy who knows when he's crossed his limit has also recorded videos saying 'Sorry, Papa' to apologize for his audacity. Not that I was ever really angry with him for his truancy; in fact, in my strictness, I also liked that he had a mind of his own, the confidence and naughtiness of a balanced child in breaking the rules to his own liking. According to me, a good education is one that fosters individuality and independent thinking, going hand-in-hand with a strong sense of responsibility. In that case, my own learning by the end of the school year has been, most importantly, the idea that I need to stop any sort of shouting for discipline and choose firmness, for aggression only serves to curb the child and does not correct his actions.

As I mentioned above, the school hours were helpful for my morning routine, but the evenings were rainy and required a lot of creativity, especially with playing in the building's compound not being a viable option. Luckily, I discovered a few warm-up videos that were suggested for physical activity at home. That did the trick and we were able to pass the evening time enjoyably and fruitfully. These energetic, child-friendly videos are challenging, though they captivated my boy with working out for more than an hour, as he took to the interactive communication and manoeuvring of obstacles on screen like a fish takes to water. The benefits were two-fold: I got to relax and enjoy my coffee while he'd be sweating it out and then he'd be so exhausted afterwards that when he went to bed, he'd go out like a light!

During these months, Laksshya started to show a new interest in music and dance, in the sense that he had a favourite song, which was 'BumBumBhole', the peppy track from the movie *3 Idiots*. It was played a lot for him and every time he heard the starting jingle, he'd move his body excitedly and wouldn't stop until the song was over. This went on like a crazy fad that lasted till we introduced him to patriotic music on 15 August, Independence Day, when he heard the classic song 'Nanha Munna Raahi Hoon' from the movie *Son of India* (1960). That became the new favourite song and continued to be his obsession for a while. During this time he'd insist on playing it repeatedly, at least five times each time the music was on, leaving his family with no other choice but to listen to it and applaud excitedly. These lockdown shenanigans, including the work that I'd done with Laksshya through that year, seemed to be having some sort of an effect in instilling a liking for the performing arts. This was also evident in school, for if you ignore the initial shyness of opening up with others, he was enjoying music and dance and went on to doing his classes independently with his own ideas, while I sat and encouraged my son.

Sunday was chosen for the asynchronous tasks, which needed various strategies to make Laksshya stop his own free play and get down to doing some schoolwork. The

DEVELOPING A PASSION FOR MUSIC

214

tasks were innovative and entertaining, like the assignment for creating different musical sounds with things at home—that was one of a kind. Likewise, there were others, too, that required the student to use sounds, movement, imagination and even singing skills for performing, to make the cut. I would get so engrossed and involved while directing him for his best potential that I'd feel like a party planner, and not exactly like a father getting homework done in the lockdown. A few months later, we had all the signs of a budding artist in Laksshya, and there was a point when he had started memorizing and singing full songs for homework and also in class for his teachers. Hallelujah!

The subsequent unlocking measures brought a ray of hope, with the outdoor areas opening up by the end of August. But there was not much rejoicing, with the kids' play area still shut. Even otherwise, hardly any of the kids showed up to play, considering the daily number of coronavirus cases in India was still rising and the peak wasn't even in sight. Luckily, the Juhu beach area was now officially open to visitors in the morning and Laksshya used to be there for almost three hours every day, like he was catching up on lost time. We also resumed a weekly class at The Little Gym, a play gym for kids, as

THE BEST MORNIN'S ARE
AT THE BEACH

that was the only real class activity that was happening and the evenings had become monotonous in our partially unlocked situation, with the warm-up videos having lost their novelty, little or no friends in the outdoor parks and, above all, the rains also acting like a major spoiler for us.

AT THE PLAY GYM AFTER THE FIRST LOCKDOWN WAS LIFTED

My writing feels so topsy-turvy at this point; I'm trying to figure out how the circumstances were changing so rapidly in the pandemic, and almost feeling blurry in my recollection of what brought relief to my son and what was still a major drag. I do remember that, by September, I was also stepping out to meet close friends once in a while. On one occasion, Laksshya asked me to call his best friend over for a play date but unfortunately the friend wasn't yet allowed to go outside and I couldn't do anything about it. That day my lad, who's otherwise very strong and adjusts to the reality of things, just broke down, asking me why his friend wasn't coming over and seeing him. What I also remember is the fact that no matter how many dull and listless times there were, both of us always picked up the pieces, cheered ourselves up and moved on with a smile.

In the constantly changing external environment, wherein balancing lives with livelihood was a priority in unlocking the economy, one never knew what was coming next and the unpredictable weather would only make us feel worse. The only constant factor that was bringing structure and normalcy to our lives were the hours of online school. At least one felt differently on a Monday or Wednesday morning from a weekend, just like in the pre-COVID days. I might seem to be exaggerating, but contrary to what many parents have been complaining about, the online programme at Laksshya's school was working out for us and I didn't feel like it was much of a compromise. Laksshya was learning concepts, like the different tastes and the manner in which the different modes of transportation work together—things that were way more important and different from what we studied in our time. He was picking up on his gardening skills for homework, using puppets to retell a story and with the dancing activities even more fun than before, thanks to ideas like the 'Move and Freeze Game', I wondered if he was losing much, even without the physical interaction in a real classroom. Maybe it's just me and my positivity, but, if you think about it, the fact that his father was present to encourage him during the school hours and monitor the asynchronous tasks like a mentor, must've only helped in enhancing his learning experience.

Realistically speaking, it's also true that no matter how well we manage our lives and the circumstances, there's only so much a child can do when the monotony of looking at a screen every day for hours begins to set in. With a delayed break for Diwali last year, Laksshya had started to get burnt out in the classes on Zoom and would resist even logging in, whenever he didn't feel like it. From leaving the study room and running to his play area, to refusing to interact with his teachers in the classes, he tried all the stunts he could

A PUPPET SHOW FOR SCHOOL

to get back to freedom. Initially I thought he was just playing truant so I'd coax him, even pick him up and get him back to the room. However, it dawned on me that he was going through online fatigue and therefore needed to get some leeway in the matter. Going forward, even in the first rehearsal for the online sports day event, after trying my best to get him to focus on the drills and failing, I gave up the effort and let him have it his way, hoping he would settle down on his own. He ignored my gestures at motivation and all the instructions of the teachers in the session, leaving me with no choice but to hold on to the mantra of optimism I was following since the pandemic had begun. His homeroom teacher agreed with the theory that his behaviour was not a problem but a passing phase, so we both decided to give him space and wait and watch.

Mercifully, during that time, a lot more things had started opening up for the rest of the day, like the LEGO classes and even our favourite evening hangout, and the outdoor parks had started buzzing with activity, a much-needed breather for my son.

Finally, the Diwali break from school had started and to add to the excitement, my passion project, *Laxmii Bomb*, renamed *Laxmii*, was also released by the digital streaming platform Disney Plus Hotstar VIP. The reviews were comme ci, comme ça, but the viewership, much to my relief, was skyrocketing. It felt like a huge responsibility that I'd been carrying for seven years was now behind me and my dream was being fulfilled. Laksshya was also meeting his friends regularly at the parks and I was letting him play until very late in the evenings, for the season of Diwali festivities in India had officially begun. The Diwali days, though, were now simpler and easier than what we were doing for years and we just stuck to all the things we wanted to do while socially distancing ourselves from crowds. My son couldn't have asked for more: he was free from his school activities, reunited with his friends, and his papa, now at his jovial best, was wrapped around his little finger. The days of positivity, light and hope for future prosperity had indeed begun.

Once the holidays were done and we were back in the structured life of school, Laksshya was raring to go, another indication of the importance of a good break in the temperament of a child. I didn't have to get pushy with my son for his online classes and he was just, quite naturally, seeking to work with his teachers and classmates a lot more. The dance and physical-education classes were suffering just before the holidays began, but now they were like his favourite hobbies. Sports-day practice, previously off to a disastrous start for Laksshya, was the first thing that he looked forward to every day. He was practising his drills and had memorized the movements of his group's performance to perfection. If I may say so myself, Laksshya was among the better performers in his class and had the right enthusiasm and confidence during the actual online sports-day event too, with a marked improvement in his skills in comparison to the previous year. What worked out for us to get to this point, where we were now enjoying our success at an online sports-day event? I think it was learning to let the child figure things out himself, a lesson in parenting that needs no introduction. However, to recognize when and how to make use of it appropriately is an art I picked up during online schooling.

It didn't take long to get into the Christmas zone of December, with another break from school awaiting the students and the vibe all around us being one of fun, play dates and Christmas parties. Yes, with COVID cases having plateaued at a certain low level, children were being allowed to step out more than before. On one occasion, we had Laksshya's schoolmates over for a play date and I remember the expression of joy on his face as he had them all together for the first time in almost a year.

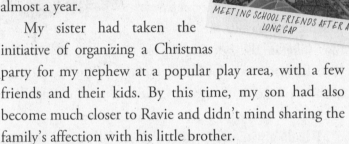

MEETING SCHOOL FRIENDS AFTER A LONG GAP

My sister had taken the initiative of organizing a Christmas party for my nephew at a popular play area, with a few friends and their kids. By this time, my son had also become much closer to Ravie and didn't mind sharing the family's affection with his little brother.

A tough year of unprecedented circumstances and struggle was coming to an end and for the resilience that we had shown in the entire rigmarole, there was good fortune in equal doses that we needed to be thankful for. So, like a reward for trailblazing through the adversities of 2020

AT THE BEACH WITH MY BROTHER

almost like they were opportunities, and for celebrating the successes in the year, my son and I took off for Mussoorie, a hill station with very few cases of COVID, to welcome the new year.

January 2021 had arrived and it looked like the new, more assertive Laksshya from the previous year was here to stay in the new year too. Like in the opening up of

IN MUSSOORIE FOR BRINGING IN 2021

COVID restrictions for India, my boy was finding pleasure in the exploration of newer avenues while rebuilding those of the time before his world was closed down.

I hadn't witnessed a more colourful side of my son before—from participating in puja ceremonies at the house to insisting on trying his hand at kite flying during the festival of Makar Sankranti and solving jigsaw puzzles with my friends. Laksshya's passion and flair for dance in school and in the class outside, which had been resumed, had me feeling like the proud father of a talented young son. If that wasn't enough, the

BACK IN FORM FOR ONLINE CLASSES

manner in which he devoured the
Wellness Wednesday tasks in the
school's midweek curriculum, which
included crafts, yoga, even cooking
and baking, was reassuring and felt
like I was doing something right
with him. And there's more to
write about.

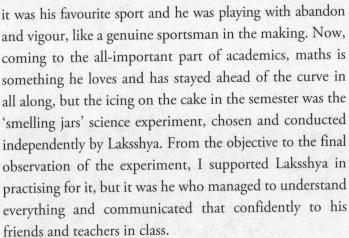

MY WELLNESS WEDNESDAY TASK FOR
THE WEEK

The soccer classes, which
resumed in February, were also
another revelation of sorts, for by now
it was his favourite sport and he was playing with abandon
and vigour, like a genuine sportsman in the making. Now,
coming to the all-important part of academics, maths is
something he loves and has stayed ahead of the curve in
all along, but the icing on the cake in the semester was the
'smelling jars' science experiment, chosen and conducted
independently by Laksshya. From the objective to the final
observation of the experiment, I supported Laksshya in
practising for it, but it was he who managed to understand
everything and communicated that confidently to his
friends and teachers in class.

We had completed almost a year in distance learning
from home and the gods must've been happier with the two
of us, for it genuinely felt like we were reaping the benefits
of our hard work together. Sorry, teachers, you've done

the unthinkable in filling the void that could've potentially made a dent in our children's educational lives, but I believe my son was flourishing owing in part to my relentlessness in making him attempt everything that was needed, by turning everything into something that he would find exciting. I'm thinking, in the process, I also learnt a lot from you guys, at least for building my own learner profile as a parent. In the IB terminology, I could say that I see myself as a more open-minded, curious and balanced parent who's also a risk-taker now. Thank you for all that. But hey, in all my pride, in case my readers are now beginning to think of me as a boastful father, I must admit that while unlocking ourselves to the world again, I felt that Laksshya had suffered in his social-skills development and I had to accept my own helplessness, given the dramatic changes in his life in the past one year. Thankfully, he was opening up to his friends in familiar surroundings, but he was now taking longer than before to warm up at parties that were outside his comfort zone. Not really a red flag for me to press the panic button, but a chilling reminder nevertheless of the work that needed to be done even after things went back to normal.

I believe that it's all a part of life and growing up in the world. Honestly, it's crazy, even otherwise, to expect children to be the most perfect version of themselves at all times. For example, Laksshya now had an attitude about playing with girls and would say, 'Boys are the best.' But he also impressed me with his self-care abilities: he had started eating, dressing up and wearing his shoes independently. The moral of the story is that we are all works in progress, aren't we? Therefore, encouraging and guiding my son in the right direction and letting him figure out the rest for himself is the best education I can give him, lockdown or no lockdown!

I just don't want to begin writing about what happened to us again in March 2021, that just when life was becoming normal again and I was planning a spring-break vacation for my son, India saw a rising count of coronavirus cases which started its rampage in Maharashtra, my home state. Really, we'd already had too much for us to feel perturbed and stressed about with the U-turn in circumstances. In fact, we were numb—no, actually, we were prepared, older, wiser and stronger, with experience in handling this virus and its mutations, and preventing them from taking us down or shaking our spirit. So, with all precautions, I took my chances and went to Dubai for Laksshya's spring break, only to be welcomed back to a growing second wave of cases in India and a whirlpool of restrictions and curfews to our freedom. My takeaway from it all was the fact that our timing was perfect and we had come back safe.

Like the Hollywood psychological thrillers of the 2000s or the 1990s comedy classic *Groundhog Day*, we found ourselves in situations very similar to 2020. School was already closed and online, but there were other last days all over again—for the parks, salons, cinemas, beaches, offices. It was a sense of complete déjà vu for me. Of course, I kept Laksshya away from the negativity in the news about COVID and planned his evenings like before, entertaining him with games like Bingo, play dates with

A MUCH-NEEDED SPRING BREAK IN DUBAI

his friends at home and a big, new trampoline to get his feet up in the air. It really pained me to see the trauma and loss of lives all over the country but for my little, simple world with my son, I found the strength to make us crawl our way into a state of happiness.

Yes, we were happy with excelling in learning about the lifecycles of living things, celebrating my dad's birthday in isolation and a new kids' fitness class with new friends, when the unlocking started, with a few curbs being eased in June.

Yes, the unlocking has restarted, with new cases of coronavirus going down every day. We're back to

GOOFY MOMENTS DURING THE LOCKDOWN

outdoor activities at least, and some sense of normalcy all over again. Nevertheless, I don't have to look too far back to see what we've already gained in the past fifteen months or so. Maturity, social responsibility, resilience, productivity, self-discovery, self-management skills, creativity, optimism, the art of letting go in parenting—this last chapter

ONLINE STUDENT–LED CONFERENCE, SHOWING ME HIS WORK PORTFOLIO

is a tribute to all the good fortune of learning and my own personal transformation in confinement. Finally, it must be my Buddhist practice and the wisdom I've gained from studying and chanting, for I also feel rejuvenated in concluding what has been the greatest source of joy and satisfaction in the last ten months, *Bachelor Dad*, my first book.

Epilogue

My journey to becoming a father has raised several questions which I have tried to address on various media platforms, though the message has often been lost in translation due to frivolous Bollywood interviews. Maybe that's why I'm feeling joyous now, because part of my objective in writing this book was to share the true picture about my life, and that will be fulfilled. The other part of the objective is not about certain big takeaways that I want people, especially parents, to learn from the book, for I am no one to advise or educate anyone about parenting through the story of my highs and lows. Every individual has his/her unique challenges and solutions that work best for the vagaries of life. What I hope to do is to inspire people to never give up believing in the fact that the answers do come, sooner or later, and it always works to wait and then follow in that direction. Trust me, after that, there's no looking back.

As for my son and I, who knows how we are going to be in the future? Our journey together has been quite unpredictable, especially how we found each other in the first place, and now within varying degrees of being locked down together for the past fifteen months or so. What we do know for sure is that we are partners, anchors to each other for life, and that is going to make the good times as well as the bad seem like opportunities—to grow together, have fun and make the most of whatever life throws at us. For the near future, in these unprecedented circumstances, I may not have space to write more, but I can see that the joyride of overcoming our challenges is ongoing, with miles to go before we really unlock.

Acknowledgements

I t's said that the best things in life just happen to us; they can never be orchestrated or planned out. *Bachelor Dad* is one such turning point to my journey thus far—it started out as an idea, but was set in motion quite accidentally, almost like the universe was conspiring to make it happen. On the other hand, they also say that there are no coincidences in this world, so from that perspective I have to give full marks to my sharp and dynamic literary agent Suhail Mathur for sensing the opportunity and getting in touch with me at the right moment, when I was hoping to write a book about my experience of becoming a single father. Many thanks to him for also guiding me on the possibilities of having a writer for my story, but above all, supporting me in my final decision to write this book independently. Thank you, The Book Bakers, for believing that I could pull off the mammoth task of writing *Bachelor*

Dad, my first book, without a co-author, for that's how I could bring another baby of my own into the world, and this time, too, singlehandedly. Thank you, author Sujata Parashar, for the title recommendation.

Sometimes, I feel like I have been tested far too much in life, but in the end I have also felt luckier than most other people, for I couldn't be more thankful for having gotten Penguin Random House India to bring such a personal memoir of my life into the public domain. Gurveen Chadha, my commissioning editor at Penguin, has been a friendly and informative support for battling the technical challenges of completing a book in the lockdowns of 2020 and 2021. She has also enhanced my work with fruitful structural changes and suggestions that speak about her excitement for the book and a personal connection with making *Bachelor Dad* loved by all. Thank you, Gurveen, for also working on the cover picture, for you made me wake up from my slumber and shoot with my son in a professional photo session, something that was long overdue. Thank you, Saloni Mital, for enhancing the writing with such a thorough and skilful edit. Last but not the least, I'm indebted to Mrs Ruprani Parikh, Ms Rutu Parikh, Mrs Firuza Parikh, Mr Prakash Jha and their families for allowing me to write about their role in my becoming a single parent. You are all heroes in this chapter of my life.

Acknowledgements

Our work is done and the book will soon be in the hands of the readers. What I can't wait for is to open a bottle of champagne with Team Penguin and Team Book Bakers, to celebrate the end of a journey that was rewarding and exhilarating, to say the least. That would also be an appropriate way to acknowledge the contribution of each other, for creating something so special to us. Until we move on to the next one, of course.